Worthington Chauncey Ford

The United States and Spain in 1790 : An episode in diplomacy described from hitherto unpublished sources

Worthington Chauncey Ford

The United States and Spain in 1790 : An episode in diplomacy described from hitherto unpublished sources

ISBN/EAN: 9783337185428

Printed in Europe, USA, Canada, Australia, Japan

Cover: Foto ©ninafisch / pixelio.de

More available books at **www.hansebooks.com**

The United States and Spain

IN 1790.

AN EPISODE IN DIPLOMACY DESCRIBED FROM
HITHERTO UNPUBLISHED SOURCES.

WITH AN INTRODUCTION BY

WORTHINGTON CHAUNCEY FORD.

BROOKLYN, N. Y.:
HISTORICAL PRINTING CLUB.
1890.

CONTENTS.

(v)

INTRODUCTION.

THE interest of the papers included in these pages lies in the light they throw upon the first question of diplomacy, which confronted the newly constituted government of the United States. During the Revolution diplomatic relations with European powers had been confined to offers of alliances, of commercial reciprocity and requests for financial aid ; but the net result had been a treaty of alliance with France, which led to important results for the revolting colonies ; a treaty of commerce with the same nation, that was entirely inoperative, thanks to the network of protective duties and prohibitions that closed the French ports to outside traders ; and a few parchments involving contracts with other nations and supposed to contain concessions that might in certain contingencies become of value, but rather from their moral and political influence, as involving a recognition of the independence of America, than from any actual bonds of interest, political or commercial. Nor had the foreign relations of the States improved during the years from the treaty of peace in 1783, to the promulgation of the new constitution and the establishment of a central government. Great Britain recognized the independence of the new nation, but refused to treat with it politically or commercially under formal exchange of ministers or a commercial treaty. The laws of trade and the rigid laws of the mercantile system gave the trade of America into British hands ;

(7)

and, enjoying a natural monopoly, the British ministry saw no good reason for jeopardizing actual profit by suggesting changes that might prove injurious. To purchase by concession what they were already in the full enjoyment of, was not recognized as good policy; nor was it more agreeable to them to open diplomatic relations that could not but lead to embarrassing controversies. There were charges of bad faith in the execution or rather evasion of the terms of the treaty of 1783, which could be judged of only by a tedious, difficult and extremely delicate weighing of claims on both sides. The Revolution in France had disarranged the relations of that people with the outside world, and already in America a feeling was engendered that a too close connection with that country might not be safe or expedient for the American interests. With Spain, there were still the embarrassing claims and denials attending the free navigation of the Mississippi; while the problem of public credit was intimately connected with the relations between the United States and their creditors—France and Holland.

This unsatisfactory condition of diplomatic relations was emphasized by the geographical bounds of the new nation. On the north was the English province of Canada, possession of which was long the object of the Continental Congress, and scattered within American territory were a number of fortified posts held and garrisoned by the British, in direct contradiction to the terms of the treaty of peace. To the south were the possessions of Spain, for whom the Americans had little affection because of the hesitating and half-hearted assistance given during the war, and because of the complications raised in the subsequent negotiations for the navigation rights of the Mississippi. When Spain in

1783 obtained both Florida and Louisiana, the Spanish government " aimed at excluding the United States, not France, from the gulf,"* and she had little compunction in showing how little regard she intended to have for the wishes of the new republic, whose very institutions implied a menace to her colonial possessions in America. The Count de Florida Blanca, now supreme in the conduct of the foreign relations of Spain, was opposed to ceding any privileges asked, much less to recognizing any rights claimed by the Americans, touching the Mississippi. Smarting under the slight inflicted by the treaty of 1783, which by a secret article looked to an English ownership of West Florida, she notified Congress that until the question of boundaries—always vexatious and easily prolonged—had been determined, the exclusive control of the Mississippi would be claimed by Spain.† As an earnest of her desire to accommodate any difference, Don Diego de Gardoqui was named "Encargado de Negocios," to reside near Congress and negotiate a settlement.

The matter might have rested there for some time had it not been for the excitement raised in the western country. The arrival of Gardoqui gave reason to look for a removal of differences and the inhabitants of the west were quite willing to await the result. But months passed and nothing was published. Jay was bound by his instructions to insist upon the right of navigation of the Mississippi from ocean to source, while Gardoqui sought to establish the views of his master by securing the exclusion of all nations—Americans included—from that part of the river that ran through his, then undefined, territory. Annoying matters were con-

---

* Henry Adams, *History of the United States*, I, 353.

† 25 June, 1784.

2

tinually arising : the unlawful occupation by Green ; and his followers of Spanish territory, an act promptly disavowed by Georgia ; the stoppage of traders at Natchez ; the question of indebtedness to Spain ; the complaints made by Indian tribes ; and what must have been most galling to Jay, the secret article of the treaty with Great Britain. At length, in August, 1786, Jay notified Congress that no treaty could be framed if the navigation right was insisted upon, and proposed to yield the claim for a period of twenty-five or thirty years, before the end of which the privilege, he thought, could hardly become of importance. *

To Madison, always firm in insisting on maintaining to the utmost the claims against Spain, such a concession was almost criminal.

" Passing by the other Southern States, figure to yourself the effect of such a stipulation on the Assembly of Virginia, already jealous of northern politics, and which will be composed of about thirty members from the western waters ; of a majority of others attached to the western country from interests of their own, of their friends, or their constituents ; and of many others who, though indifferent to Mississippi, will zealously play off the disgust of their friends against Federal measures. Figure to yourself its effect on the people at large on the western waters, who are impatiently waiting for a favorable result to the negotiation of Gardoqui, and who will consider themselves as sold by their Atlantic brethren. Will it be an unnatural consequence if they con-

---

* " With respect to the Spaniards, I do not think the navigation of the Mississippi is an object of great importance to us at *present ;* and when the banks of the Ohio and the fertile plains of the western country get thickly inhabited, the people will embrace the advantages which nature affords them in spite of all opposition." *Washington to Rochambeau,* 7 September, 1785.

sider themselves absolved from every Federal tie, and court some protection for their betrayed rights? This protection will appear more attainable from the maritime power of Britain than from any other quarter; and Britain will be more ready than any other nation to seize an opportunity of embroiling our affairs. . . . I should rather suppose that he [the Spanish minister] means to work a total separation of interest and affection between. western and eastern settlements, and to foment the jealousy between eastern and southern States. By the former, the population of the western country, it may be expected, will be checked, and the Mississippi so far secured; and, by both, the general security of Spanish America be promoted."*

This expression of an extreme view was actually a very accurate forecast of what did occur, so far as it applied to the inhabitants of the western country. A rough population, having no sentimental ties that could bind them to home or state, by necessity often trespassers or aggressors, using force to obtain what they thought belonged to them, adventurous and restless, easily influenced by a desire for gain that need not respect the shadowy claims of a government incapable of enforcing them, and captivated by the energy and promises of demagogues, it was not to be expected that they would fret long under the restraints imposed upon them by Spain, acting through her governors on the Mississippi. Retaliation was the readiest weapon at hand. Green, who had already figured as the Governor of a State parcelled out of Spanish territory, came again to the front, and another adventurer, Clark, in return for a seizure by the Spanish at Natchez, rifled a Spanish trader's store at Vincennes. If the Americans were not permitted to trade down

---

* *Madison to Jefferson*, 12 August, 1786.

the river, it was urged the Spaniards should not trade up. And a vigorously expressed protest now appeared which did much to excite a public feeling against the Spaniards, as well as against the Congress :

COPY OF A LETTER FROM A GENTLEMAN AT THE FALLS OF OHIO TO HIS FRIEND IN NEW ENGLAND, DATED DECEMBER 4, 1786.

Dear Sir : Politics, which a few months ago were scarcely thought of, are now sounded aloud in this part of the world, and discussed by almost every person. The late commercial treaty with Spain, in shutting up, as it is said, the navigation of the Mississippi for the term of twenty-five years, has given this western country a universal shock, and struck its inhabitants with amazement. Our foundation is affected ; it is therefore necessary that every individual exert himself to apply a remedy. To sell and make us vassals to the merciless Spaniards is a grievance not to be borne. The Parliamentary acts which occasioned our revolt from Great Britain were not so barefaced and intolerable. To give us the liberty of transporting our effects down the river to New Orleans, and then be subject to the Spanish laws and impositions, is an insult upon our understanding. We know, by woful experience, that it is in their power, when once there, to take our produce at any price they please. Large quantities of flour, tobacco, meal, &c., have been taken there the last summer, and mostly confiscated : those who had permits from their Governor were obliged to sell at a price he was pleased to state, or subject themselves to lose the whole. Men of large property are already ruined by their policy. What benefit can you on the Atlantic shores receive from this act? The Spaniards, from the amazing resources of this river, can supply all their own markets at a much lower price than you possibly can. Though this country has been settling but about six years, and that in the midst of an inveterate enemy, and most of the first adventurers fallen a prey to the savages, and although the emigration to this country is so rapid that the internal market is very great, yet the quantity of produce they now have on hand is immense. Flour and pork are now selling here at twelve shillings the hundred; beef in proportion; any quantities of Indian corn can be had at ninepence per bushel. Three times the quantity of tobacco and corn can be raised on an acre here that can be within the settlement on the east side of the mountains, and with less cultivation. It is, therefore, rational to suppose that, in a very few years, the vast bodies of water in those rivers will labor under the immense weight of the produce of this rich and fertile country, and Spanish ships be unable to convey it to market. Do you think to prevent the emigration from a barren country, loaded with taxes and impoverished with debts, to the most luxurious and fertile soil in the world? Vain is the thought and presumptuous the supposition. You may as well endeavor to prevent the fishes from gathering on a bank in the sea which affords them plenty of nourishment. Shall the best and largest part of the United States be uncultivated, a nest for savages and beasts of prey? Certainly not. Providence has designed it for some nobler purposes. This is convincing to every one who beholds the many advantages and pleasing prospects of this country. Here is a soil richer to appearance than can possibly be made by art; large plains and meadows, without the labor of hands, sufficient to support millions of cattle summer and winter; cane, which is also a fine nourishment for them, without bounds. The spontaneous production of this country surpasses your imagination; consequently I see nothing to prevent our herds being as numerous here, in time, as they are in the Kingdom of Mexico. Our lands to the northward of Ohio, for the produce of wheat, &c., will, I think, vie with the Island of Sicily. Shall all this country now be cultivated entirely for the use of the Spaniards? Shall we be their bondmen, as the children of Israel were to the Egyptians? Shall one part of the United States be slaves while the other is free? Human nature shudders at the thought, and freemen will despise those who could be so mean as to even contemplate on so vile a subject.

Our situation is as bad as it possibly can be ; therefore, every exertion to retrieve our circumstances must be manly, eligible, and just.

We can raise twenty thousand troops this side the Alleghany and Appalachian mountains ; and the annual increase of them by emigration from other parts is from two to four thousand.

We have taken all the goods belonging to the Spanish merchants of post Vincennes and the Illinois, and are determined they shall not trade up the river, provided they will not let us trade down it. Preparations are now making here (if necessary) to drive the Spaniards from their settlements at the mouth of the Mississippi. In case we are not countenanced and succored by the United States, (if we need it,) our allegiance will be thrown off, and some other Power applied to. Great Britain stands ready with open arms to receive and support us ; they have already offered to open their resources for our supplies. When once reunited to them, "farewell, a long farewell, to all your boasted greatness ;" the province of Canada and the inhabitants of these waters, of themselves, in time, will be able to conquer you. You are as ignorant of this country as Great Britain was of America. These hints, if rightly improved, may be of some service ; if not, blame yourselves for the neglect.

The anti-federal sentiments shown in such expressions of opinion naturally disturbed Madison, and he returned to the Continental Congress with the intention of forcing the question of the Mississippi, now by a legislative trick, as he thought, left almost entirely in the hands of Jay. He was supported in this by the strong feeling of the Virginia Legislature, asserting in unmistakable language the importance of acquiring the right of navigating the river. But he was opposed by the indifference, or rather the interest, of the Eastern and some of the Middle States. To them, the navigation of the western river meant nothing ; for they were more intent upon acquiring commercial privileges in the Spanish West Indies, and were willing, almost eager, to secure these at the expense of the claims applying to the Mississippi. It was on the vote of the four Eastern States, with the assistance of New York, New Jersey and Pennsylvania, that the restriction imposed upon Jay in his negotiations, of insisting upon this right, had been repealed ; and this vote was based upon such motives as were not likely to be changed. For New York saw in the west a rival to her commercial interests, and Pennsylvania, if not controlled, was at least influenced, by the same jealousy. In 1786 the feeling was so strong as to produce a talk of separation of the Middle and Eastern States from the Southern, should a determination of the matter be forced, and conclude to the injury of the wishes of the former. * Yet, as Madison said, would the Eastern States have remained quiet under a cession by Congress of the fishery rights for commercial privileges applying to tobacco? To yield the navigation rights in exchange for liberty to export fish and flour into the Spanish colonies involved, in his view, as great a sectional sacrifice, the South and West being sacrificed to the North. †

---

* *Monroe to Madison*, 3 September, 1786.

† Early in his negotiations, Gardoqui had said that as the Spanish King " has no occasion for the codfish, oil, salmon, grain, flour, rice, nor other productions, he may, considering the right which obliges his subjects to provide themselves by their own industry or other useful and important means, find it convenient to prohibit them, to remind this nation [*i. e.* the United States] at present, as a friend, that they have no treaty." *Gardoqui to Jay*, 25 May, 1786.

The threatening situation in the West, however, did produce a change of sentiment. New Jersey instructed her delegates in Congress to labor for the navigation, while a change in the Pennsylvania representation gave her vote to the South. Rhode Island, believing an extensive land speculation was under the apparent indifference of her New England sister States, added her influence to the same side. Gorham of Massachusetts bluntly expressed the selfishness of the East by avowing his wish to close the Mississippi, that the inducements to move into the western country might be lessened, and the drain on the population and wealth of the Atlantic States thereby decreased. In spite of this, the Spanish agent gained the impression that the general drift of American policy was opposed to insisting on the right, and he urged this upon his court. * Here the matter rested, for the institution of a new government took it out of the hands of the confederation, and gave it, with a legacy of other undetermined questions, to the newly formed administration of President Washington.

In the *Washington Papers* are full summaries in the President's writing of the correspondence between Jay and Gardoqui, but without note or comment. Nor is there to be found any note or memorandum to show whether there was any special incident in the west, or on the Mississippi, or in Spain, that should have brought this question before

---

* " It appears to me now, as it has long done, that they think here a free port on the Mississippi will satisfy the wishes of the Americans, and on that idea ground their expectations that the instructions sent in autumn last to Mr. Gardoqui will enable that gentleman to bring the negotiations to a speedy termination." *Carmichael to Jay*, 29 April, 1788.

the Cabinet. In August, 1790, the matter was taken up, and the various steps taken are detailed in the following pages.

The instruments at hand for conducting a negotiation were few and imperfect. Gardoqui had returned to Spain, leaving his secretary José Ignacio de Viar, in charge, while Carmichael, as merely *chargé* at the Court of Madrid, found it difficult to secure access to Florida Blanca, and was compelled to depend more upon a certain "back-door" influence than upon his own activity. The United States had no diplomatic representative in England, but Gouverneur Morris was there in an unofficial capacity, seeking to pave the way for a settlement of differences and an exchange of ministers. Jefferson, whose long service abroad would have rendered his assistance valuable in a negotiation, was the Secretary of State, and forced to depend upon such agents as the infant diplomatic system of the government were supplied with. In Portugal, closely connected with Spain in everything but policy, there was no American representative, and in France there was nothing higher than a *chargé d' affaires*. On the other hand, the Netherlands was the only European power that had a minister resident regularly accredited to the United States, and France was the only power that could supply a means of diplomatic communication so high as a *chargé d' affaires*—Otto. While the European courts were fully cognizant of every step taken by the American agents in Europe, and had an almost immediate knowledge of all that they proposed, Jefferson acted on imperfect knowledge, gained often from doubtful sources, and secured long after the events described had happened, when new combinations might have produced new situations. Six weeks were required for the passage of a letter from London to New York, nine weeks were a fair run from Paris, and sometimes nineteen weeks elapsed between the delivery of a letter by a *chargé* and its receipt by Jefferson. Nor was this the only drawback, for it was reasonably certain that before Carmichael's letters could leave Spain, or Jefferson's be delivered to him, the Spanish court had read them and were perfectly cognizant of what they contained. Even the cypher used between these two was known to it.

A new danger to the United States appeared in the prospect of war between Spain and Great Britain, in the event of which a contest between the two powers in America was most probable, as the weakness of the Spanish colonies offered a tempting prize to the power of a nation almost supreme on the ocean. The Spaniards had laid claim to nearly the whole of the western coast of America, from Cape Horn to the sixtieth degree of north latitude, and had watched with a feeling of jealousy, aggravated by a sense of injury, the establishment of a British settlement in Nootka Sound, on Vancouver's Island. This inlet of the sea had been first explored by Captain Cook in one of his voyages, and, on the establishment of the English in India, became a trading station, colonized by the English and recognized by grants of land from the natives. After three years of undisturbed possession, the little settlement was surprised by the arrival of two Spanish ships of war from Mexico, which seized an English merchant vessel—the Iphigenia—imprisoned her crew, looted the vessel, and pulling down the British flag on the settlement, raised that of Spain, and subsequently treated all comers as intruders.

Spain, while recognizing that she had committed an aggravated insult upon the English flag, was at first inclined to to assume a high position, demanding that British subjects should in the future refrain from trespassing on Spanish territory ; but, in consideration of the "ignorance" of those who had landed at Nootka, the seized vessels were released. Such a message was little suited to the disposition of Pitt or of the English people, and in default of further reparation from Spain, war must ensue, for which extensive preparations were made on both sides.

The Spanish were collecting their fleets at Cadiz and Ferrol, and the king on May 5, 1790, announced to Parliament the prospect of war. A credit was given, but little opposition appeared ; and while a peaceable settlement was sought by sending a negotiator—Mr. Alleyne Fitzherbert *—to Madrid, with instructions to insist on a full reparation to the injured, before consenting even to a discussion of the abstract rights involved, the collection of an army, fleets and munitions of war was actively pushed, and plans formed for · attacking Spain in the West Indies and South America.

The news of the King's message reached the United States in June, and was, as Jefferson termed it, "interesting news." The aggressiveness of Great Britain was acknowledged. "You will see by the papers enclosed that Great Britain is itching for war. I do not see how one can be avoided, unless Spain should be frightened into concessions. The con-

---

* Fitzherbert had been sent to Paris in 1782 to negotiate the treaty of peace between Great Britain and France and Spain ; and it was for his services in bringing to a successful end the negotiations with Spain on the Nootka question, that he was raised to the Irish peerage as Baron St. Helen's.

sequences of such an event must have an important relation to the affairs of the United States."* "It was evident
they [the British Houses of Parliament] would accept
nothing short of an extensive renunciation from Spain as to
her American pretensions. Perhaps she is determined to
be satisfied with nothing but war, dismemberment of the
Spanish empire, and annihilation of her fleet. Nor does
her countenance towards us clear up at all."† But there
might be a compensation to America. "If the war between
France and Spain takes place, I think France will inevit-
ably be involved in it. In that case, I hope the new world
will fatten on the follies of the old. If we can but establish
the armed neutrality for ourselves, we must become the
carriers for all parties as far as we can raise vessels."‡
Washington, just recovered from an illness that had almost
proved fatal, made the first mention of the possibility of
the Floridas being involved in the threatened war, but insisted on the policy of neutrality. "It seems to be our
policy to keep in the situation in which nature has placed
us, to observe a strict neutrality, and to furnish others with
those good things of subsistence which they may want, and
which our fertile land abundantly produces, if circumstances
and events will permit us to do so. . . . Gradually recovering from the distresses in which the war left us, patiently
advancing in our task of civil government, unentangled in
the crooked politics of Europe, wanting scarcely anything
but the full navigation of the Mississippi (which we must

* *Madison to Pendleton*, 22 June, 1790.

† *Jefferson to Monroe*, 20 June, 1790.

‡ *Jefferson to E. Rutledge*, 4 July, 1790.

have, and as certainly shall have as we remain a nation), I have supposed, that, with the undeviating exercise of a just, steady and prudent national policy, we shall be the gainers, whether the powers of the old world may be in peace or war, but more especially in the latter case. In that case our importance will certainly increase, and our friendship be courted. Our dispositions will not be indifferent to Britain or Spain. Why will not Spain be wise and liberal at once? It would be easy to annihilate all causes of quarrels between that nation and the United States at this time. At a future period, that may be far from being a fact. Should a war take place between Great Britain and Spain, I conceive, from a great variety of concurring circumstances, there is the highest probability that the Floridas will soon be in the possession of the former."*

In these phrases were compressed the policy of the government : neutrality, if possible, and an attempt to make the difference between the European powers a means of obtaining concessions from Spain long sought for. "The part we are to act," wrote Jefferson to Carmichael, "is uncertain, and will be difficult. The unsettled state of our dispute with Spain, may give a turn to it very different from what we would wish,"—and Col. David Humphreys was sent to Madrid to aid Carmichael, bearing a sketch of general matters to be considered in the negotiation, drawn up by Jefferson. † In introducing Humphreys to Carmichael, Jefferson wrote :—

"With this information, written and oral, you will be en-

---

* *Washington to Lafayette*, 11 August, 1790.

† *Post.*

abled to meet the minister in conversations on the subject of the navigation of the Mississippi, to which we wish you to lead his attention immediately. Impress him thoroughly with the necessity of an early and even an immediate settlement of this matter, and of a return to the field of negotiation for this purpose ; and though it must be done delicately, yet he must be made to understand unequivocally, that a resumption of the negotiation is not desired on our part, unless he can determine, in the first opening of it, to yield the immediate and full enjoyment of that navigation. . . . It is impossible to answer for the forbearance of our western citizens. We endeavor to quiet them with the expectation of an attainment of their rights by peaceable means. But should they, in a moment of impatience, hazard others, there is no saying how far we may be led ; for neither themselves nor their rights will ever be abandoned by us.

"You will be pleased to observe, that we press these matters warmly and firmly, under this idea, that the war between Spain and Great Britian will be begun before you receive this ; and such a moment must not be lost. But should an accommodation take place, we retain, indeed, the same object and the same resolutions unalterably ; but your discretion will suggest, that in that event they must be pressed more softly, and that patience and persuasion must temper your conferences, till either these may prevail, or some other circumstance turn up, which may enable us to use other means for the attainment of an object which we are determined, in the end, to obtain at every risk."*

In the event of war the good offices of France, to assist in the negotiations at Madrid, were to be asked.†

In his rough draft of "Heads of Consideration" for Mr. Carmichael, drawn up by Jefferson 2 August, 1790, the possibility of a necessary coalition with Great Britain against

---

*Jefferson to Carmichael, 2 August, 1790.

† Jefferson to William Short, 10 August, 1790.

Spain was considered. The inhabitants of the western country required a vent for their surplus products, and the natural vent was down the Mississippi. To deny the privilege of navigating that river to the mouth to the Americans, was to invite a complication not easily to be solved. Either the federal government must take up the cause of the western people and by force or negotiation obtain concessions from Spain ; or it must reduce the Kentuckians to an acquiescence in the arbitrary decrees of Spain ; or it must consent to a separation of the western territory. To abandon the west or reduce it to obedience was equally impracticable, and it remained only to obtain concesssions. If by force, the United States could act alone or in conjunction with Great Britain "with a view to partition," and in the latter case Jefferson noted :

"The Floridas (includg N. Orleans) would be assigned to us. Louisiana (or all the country on the westn waters of ye Missi.) to them. We confess that such an alliance is not what we would wish, because it may eventually lead us into embarrassing situations as to our best friend, and put the power of two n'bors into ye hands of one. Ld Lansdowne has declared he gave the Floridas to Spain rather than to the U. S., as a bone of discord with the H. of Bourbon, and of reunion with Gr. Br. Connolly's attempt (as well as other facts) prove they keep it in view." *

The English and Spanish negotiations were continued through the summer. On June 4th the Spanish ministry declared that the release of the vessels had been a sufficient reparation for actual injury, and there only remained the

---

* This document is printed in full *post.*

question of right to be determined, a question that the instructions to Fitzherbert prevented him from discussing under such a declaration. The English demanded a restoration of the vessels, a full indemnity for the seizure, and a reparation for the insult committed on the English flag. Count de Florida Blanca replied that he would grant the satisfaction demanded, on condition that the damages were determined by an impartial judge, and that all the rights of Spain should be positively reserved. (June 18.) England continued her preparations and called upon Holland to assist her, as she was bound to by treaty. In response a Dutch fleet joined Admiral Howe at Portsmouth, and as a counter-movement Spain collected a fleet at Cadiz.

Nor did Spain stand alone in the matter, for by the *pacte de famille* France was bound to give her assistance in an offensive or defensive war, and notice that such aid might become necessary was served upon the French ministry. Coming as it did, when France was in the throes of revolution, it naturally produced some difference of opinion, with which questions of constitutional policy were commingled. A few months before, Mirabeau had induced the Assembly to decide that while the right of peace and war belonged to the nation, war could be declared only by a decree of the Assembly based upon a formal and pressing (*nécessaire*) proposal of the king, and approved by him. The legislature, by controlling the supplies, could at any time, even in the progress of a war, impose the necessity of making peace upon the king. Such a decision need not have proved embarrassing had not the country been bound to perform certain acts, under certain contingencies, and apparently without the power of questioning their justice or expediency. The "Society of 1789," where, as in the "Club des Jacobins," questions of public policy were discussed before being submitted to the Assembly, declared that it was impossible to maintain the "family compact" under the existing constitution. " They say that they cannot adhere to engagements which never were just, which are incompatible with the rights of man and the principles of a free constitution, and which render the nation dependent upon the will of one man, and that man a stranger. They declare such treaties between kings to be conspiracies against the people of their respective countries." *

. So distinctly colored as was this declaration with the temper of the time as to be almost grotesque, Mirabeau was too shrewd a politician not to recognize that it represented such a share of public opinion that it could not wisely be ignored. He knew the advantage of preserving the Spanish alliance, yet that alliance must be modified to make it conform better with the prevalent ideas of the universal brotherhood of man, and also to render it palatable to those who looked upon it as an instrument of monarchy —a euphemism for tyranny. Besides, France herself had important colonial interests in the West Indies, whose safety would be jeopardized by a rupture of peace with Great Britain. Spain had served notice that she would look elsewhere for alliances, should France fail her, and demanded an immediate state of the conduct the ministers intended to pursue. It was Mirabeau who drew up the report expressing the opinion of the Comité Diplomatique on the compact, and who laid it before the Assembly on the 25th of August. Earl Gower wrote of it :—

---

* Dispatches of Earl Gower, 9 July, 1790.

3

"It consisted in advising the Assembly to empower them to examine that treaty in order to form out of it a national compact, by leaving out all the articles offensive, and at the same time to request the king to order his minister at the Court of Madrid to enter into a negotiation with the Spanish ministry upon those grounds. They proposed two decrees :

" 1st. That all existing treaties shall be maintained by the French nation until it shall have revised and modified them.

" 2nd. That, before the thorough examination of treaties which the nation may think proper to continue or alter, the king shall be requested to make known to all the powers with which France is connected that justice and the love of peace are the bases of the French constitution ; that the nation cannot admit in her treaties any stipulations which are not purely defensive and commercial. That accordingly they request the king to inform his Catholic Majesty that the French nation, in taking all proper measures to maintain peace, will abide by the engagements which her government has contracted with Spain. That they also desire the king to order his ministers to negotiate accordingly with the Court of Spain, and to commission thirty ships of the line, eight of which at least to be fitted out in the ports of the Mediterranean.

"This report was taken into consideration yesterday morning, and, after a short debate, the Assembly decreed that they would abide by the defensive and commercial engagements which the government has contracted with Spain ; that the king should be desired to order his ambassadors to negotiate with the ministers of the Catholic king in order to strengthen, by a national treaty, tyes useful to both people, and to fix with precision and clearness all stipulations which may not be entirely conformable to the views of general peace and to the principles of justice, which shall always be the politics of the French ; and also, taking into consideration the armaments of the different nations of Europe, their progressive increase, the security of the French colonies and commerce, they decreed that the king shall be desired to order into commission forty-five ships of the line, with a proportionable number of frigates and small vessels."

These acts, a curious mixture of politics and sentiment, were what appeared on the surface, and while seeking to retain the expectancy of Spain for aid by a vote for ships, delay was also the object. Nor was this all. The preparations of England on so large a scale, to secure what was regarded as a very disproportionate end, could not but arouse the suspicions of the continental nations that some other object was to be attained. Late in July the *Journal des Débats et Décrets* said : " Il est impossible aussi que ces armemens regard l' Espagne seule. Il est bien probable qu'elles ménacent également les possessions Françoises."* Such a view was promptly disavowed by the French ministry ; but England knew the terms of the family compact, and could not fail to be irritated by the vote of the Assembly to increase the navy, though assured by M. Montmorin that the increase would be very gradual, and by both M. Montmorin and M. Neckar of the desire of France for peace. Earl Gower was instructed to notify the French ministry that "any assistance offered to Spain will oblige the British Cabinet to adopt such measures as may be most likely to render that assistance ineffectual ;" and to still further support England's position, Hugh Elliott was sent on a secret mission to France. It is to Mr. Oscar Browning that our knowledge of his mission is due, and we quote his note :—

---

* Even in England the good faith of the ministry in asking for a credit to arm against Spain was questioned, for there had already existed a belief that an expedition to the Baltic was on foot.

"Pitt was using the strongest and most haughty language to compel Spain to submit to us, but if France joined her these remonstrances would be ineffectual, and a European war would break out. Mirabeau was not a minister, and therefore Lord Gower could have no communication with him, but he was chairman of the *comité diplomatique* of the National Assembly, in whose hands, rather than in those of the minister, lay the issues of peace and war. It was important to secure that Mirabeau should not only maintain the principle that France was not bound to assist Spain under the present circumstances, but should do all he could to urge Spain to submit to the demands of England. If Elliott was authorized to use any other arguments to Mirabeau of a more delicate or secret nature, it would be a reason for the correspondence having completely disappeared."

Whatever were the arguments used, they were so effective that the popular party signified to Lord Gower "their earnest desire to use their influence with the Court of Madrid in order to bring it to accede to the just demands of his Majesty, and, if supported by us, I am induced to believe they will readily prefer an English alliance to a Spanish compact."*

Count de Florida Blanca in the meantime was losing heart. His efforts to secure the aid of France had resulted in an apparent acquiescence, it is true, but the widespread disaffection and mutiny in the French fleet and army would make the aid an element of danger rather than of strength. He had coquetted with the United States by throwing out a hint that the right to navigate the Mississippi might be conceded,†—this to prevent the possible alliance between the

---

* *Gower's Despatches*, 22 October, 1790.

†On September 21st, Hamilton wrote to Washington speaking of a

United States and Great Britain. His own position was precarious, and to serve as a figure-head for executing the policy of another and irresponsible person, was not kind to his temper. He thought it best to yield. "Je me rends á vos conditions," he said to Fitzhebert, "non parce qu'elles sont justes, mais parce que j'y suis forcé. Si la France nous avait aidé, je ne m'y serais jamais soumis, mais nous ne pouvons tout seuls nous mesures avec nous. Faites donc ce que vous voulez." On the 28th October the convention was signed, "by which it was agreed that the lands and buildings of which British subjects had been dispossessed in North America should be restored to them ; that British subjects should not be disturbed or molested in carrying on their fisheries in the South Seas, or in making settlements for the purpose of commerce on the coasts of those seas in places not already occupied ; and that on the other hand the

---

letter from Daniel Parker, dated London, the 12th of July, which men-tioned that " he had just seen M. de Miranda, who had recently con-versed with the Marquis del Campo, from whom he learned that the Court of Spain had acceded to our right of navigating the Mississippi. Col. Smith has also read to me a passage out of another letter of the 6th of July, which mentions that orders had been sent to the Viceroy of Mexico and the Governor of New Orleans not to interrupt the passage of vessels of the United States through that river."

On September 22d Lear, in a letter to the President, announced it a based on "pretty direct information," and the letter of Gouverneu Morris dated 2 July, reporting that the concession was "matter of com-mon report," must have been in the President's hands for some time Further than this, Lear in New York and King in Boston claimed to have authentic information of a full accommodation between Grea Britain and Spain—a premature conclusion, based upon mere rumors. See also Humphreys' letter, *post*.

king of Britain should engage to take the most effectual measures that these fisheries should not be made a pretext for illicit trade with the Spanish settlements; and with that view it was further stipulated that British subjects should not carry on their fisheries within ten leagues from any part of the coast already occupied by Spain."*

This convention was used by the United States as a precedent when urging its claims in the Oregon question.

Congress adjourned on August 12th, and on the 15th the President, accompanied by Jefferson, started on a journey to Rhode Island which occupied about ten days. On their return to New York the President addressed a series of questions to the Vice-President, the Chief Justice and the three members of his Cabinet, on the position to be taken should Lord Dorchester, † the Governor of Quebec, wish to strike the Spanish colonies by sending troops from Detroit, through the territory of the United States. It is the replies to these questions that are printed in the following pages, and constitute the first discussion in diplomacy by Washington's advisers that we have a record of. The documents speak for themselves, and the subsequent events may now be described. Although such an application was never formally made, the replies have an interest when brought into comparison with Jefferson's negotiations with France and Spain during his presidency, which led up to the purchase of Louisiana.

---

* Stanhope, *Life of Pitt*, II, 62. The convention determining the indemnity was made in February, 1793, and the port at Nootka was not evacuated by the Spanish until 1795.

† Better known as General Guy Carleton. He was created Baron Dorchester in 1786.

Humphreys, after a tempestuous passage of five weeks, reached London on the morning of October 14, and found that the confident tone the ministry had adopted in the summer had altered. A feeling prevailed that Spain was artfully putting off a settlement while sounding the attitude of France, and the prospect of her assistance in case of actual war.* Still war seemed more probable than peace; the stock market was uncertain, insurance was at war premium, the press gang was still at work, and all the usual preparations for war were being pushed. "While the powers of Europe are in such a political ferment, America is daily growing of more importance in their view. A report has prevailed in this place that Spain has lately made some declaration, with respect to conceding to the United States the free navigation of the Mississippi. I took considerable pains to trace it, and yesterday was told Col.† Miranda had seen it in a letter to the Spanish ambassador himself. My informant received the intelligence from Miranda." ‡ Six Cherokee chiefs came to London, "as ambassadors from a nation which (according to the English printed communication) has 20,000 men in arms ready to assist G. Britain against Spain"—an assertion as ludicrous as it was preposterous. Up to the hour of his leaving England—4 November—Humphreys was unable to say whether the complication would terminate in peace or war, although the convention with Spain had then been signed nearly a week (28 October), and the immediate end of his mission to Spain

---

* *Humphreys to the Secretary of State*, London, 14 October, 1790.

† Count.

‡ *Humphreys to the Secretary of State*, 20 October, 1790.

rendered abortive. On reaching Lisbon, two weeks later, he learned of the agreement, and in vague terms of the details covered.

Humphreys, however, determined to go to Madrid, and leaving Lisbon on the 3d of December he reached the Spanish capital on the 17th, after a tedious journey, travelling from daylight to dark, and making but one stop about an hour in the middle of the day. The convention was then being "partially circulated," printed on a single sheet in Spanish and French,* but for nearly two weeks the special messenger sent no dispatch to the American Secretary of State. On the 3d of January, 1791, he broke silence and in cipher wrote to Jefferson :—

[In cipher]

MADRID, 3 January, 1791.

I have had, sir, many conversations with Mr. Carmichael on the subject of your letter to him. If it had arrived early in summer, he thinks we might have obtained all our wishes. Then the critical state of affairs induced the Comte de Florida Blanca to throw out those general assertions that we should have no reason to complain of the conduct of this Court, with respect to the Mississippi, which gave rise to the report its navigation was opened. That minister had intimations from del Campo of the conferences between Mr. Morris and the Duke of Leeds, which occasioned him to say with warmth to Mr. Carmichael, now is your time to make a treaty with England. Fitzherbert availed himself of those conferences to create apprehensions that the Americans would aid his nation in case of war. Long time the conduct of Spain was fluctuating and undecided. After a variety of circumstances (which Mr. Carmichael has explained in his dispatches that have miscarried, and which he

---

* Humphreys to the Secretary of State, Madrid, 18 December, 1790.

will repeat in others by me) a convention was formed whereby the British gained substantially everything they at first demanded. Want of money to support a war and the Queen's intrigues, together with advice from the Comte Montemorin that peace was essential to France, were probably the principal causes which compelled Spain to yield the point after each side had tried which could hold out the longest. The preparations cost Spain sixteen millions dollars. Thus the crisis most favorable for the attainment of our wishes is past. Unless there is some secret article in the Convention by which England guarantees the possessions of Spain in America, resentment may [*indecipherable*] in the Spanish Court for having been obliged to receive the law. They may also desire to be in readiness for events. How far these or other motives may operate in producing change of system with respect to the United States, remains to be learnt from an adherence to the latter part of your instructions to Mr. Carmichael.

The fact is clear that the United States are daily gaining political consideration in Europe. Spain, guided by narrow policy towards its colonies, fears the consequence of our increasing strength and resources. The Compte de Florida Blanca has been so long and so obstinately opposed to the admission of foreign vessels into the Gulf of Mexico, that the most he can ever be persuaded to do, will be to suffer somebody else to negotiate, to whom, if there be blame for inconsistency in policy, the fault may be imputed. But the Compte not being well with the Queen, loses credit; and recent circumstances indicate that he is but the ostensible, while le Rena (at the head of the finance) is the real minister. Mr. Carmichael thinks, that if the Compte will not consent to open a negotiation with liberal views, it may be possible to displace him and find a successor of better dispositions : that is, if the Queen lives, but she is apprehensive of dying in childbed next month, which event would give the Compte more weight than ever. Campomanes, who is the head of the judicators, Compte de Aranda, and .many others, entertain just ideas with respect to our country. The first is high in influence and secretly an enemy to the Compte de Florida Blanca; the last, at the head of opposition, will not come into office himself, but, in case of a change of administration, some of his friends will succeed. Mr. Carmichael, being on terms of intimacy with the characters here, is certainly capable of effecting more at this Court than any other American. . . .

Something also gives uneasiness to this Court. Affairs do not go well. Frequent councils are convened. The government is feeble, jealous, mercenary and unpopular. The King is a well-disposed, passionate, weak man. The Queen (a shrewd, well-instructed woman, addicted to pleasure and expense) governs the kingdom. She is not beloved. Nor did either of them receive the usual acclamations of the people when they returned from their country residence last fall. The Queen has even been insulted, which makes her appear rarely in public. For this offense twelve washerwomen have been confined, and their husbands banished the kingdom, because they petitioned for their release. Several natives of distinction have lately been exiled from the capital to the provinces, among others the Comptesse of Galvez. Compte Segur, a Frenchman accused of being the author of a libel against the Queen, within a week past died of rigorous confinement. This government, alarmed at the success of the revolution in France, shows great distrust and hatred of the French. Several have been arrested at midnight and hurried out of the country. People begin to think and even to speak in private circles freely. In some provinces dissatisfaction prevails on account of new taxes. Three regiments are just sent into Gallicia to quell those disturbances, where an attempt was made to assassinate the new general on the road. General Lacy (who commands at Barcelona and has been obliged to menace the city by turning the cannon against it) is continually writing to Court for men and military supplies. Tho' the Spaniards in many places retain the appearance, habits and manners of a people who have but lately lost their liberty, yet affairs are not ripe for reformation, from want of leaders, information and means of combination. The utmost diligence is used to suppress intelligence from other countries. Notwithstanding I had the necessary passports, at the frontier town I was delayed a day and not permitted to proceed, until the officers of police had put my letters under cover to the police in Madrid. This having been done in my presence, they delivered them to me, with an apology for the strictness of their orders. On my arrival at Madrid, I went directly to Mr. Carmichael, and upon his application to the Compte de Florida Blanca, the letters (which had remained in my trunk under the seal of government,) were returned unopened into my hand. But notwithstanding all precautions, letters, newspapers and pamphlets come from France into this kingdom. Interesting paragraphs are copied, circulated, and read with avidity. . . .

[In Cipher]

MADRID, 15 January, 1791.

Sir: I have employed my time here in communicating according to instructions the sentiments of the President on the navigation of the Mississippi, and other important points. Mr. Carmichael's ideas are just ; his exertions will be powerful and unremitting to obtain the accomplishment of our desires before his departure from this country ; the task will now be difficult, if not impracticable, from the opinions which are impressed on this court. I fear these are rather riveted than impressed to the very substance of their former jealous policy. I learn from other good authority, as well as from Mr. Carmichael, that all the representations of Gardoqui (when minister in America) tended to excite a belief that the most respectable and influential people throughout the United States did not wish to have the navigation of the Mississippi opened for years to come, from an apprehension that such an event would weaken the government, and impoverish the Atlantic States by emigrations. It was even pre-

tended that none but a handful of settlers on the western
waters, and a few inhabitants of the southern states, would
acquiesce in the measure.

At present affairs here are guided more by intrigue than
by reason. So that no one can answer for the consequence
of a negotiation. Means are used to bring our subject with
advantage into discussion. The king is just gone to hunt
for two days; play is usual after the holidays; his prime
minister and the family ambassadors only attended him.
Nothing can be ascertained until his return.

It is not improbable a change of ministry may soon take
place. The situation about the Court becomes every day
more critical. Nor is it less so in the country. The night
before last, twenty-two French and Italians were sent from
Madrid under guard, out of the kingdom, for speaking too
freely; as was one Spanish Marquis to a distant province.
. . .

For nine days longer Humphreys remained in Madrid in
the character of a traveller, hoping that Carmichael could
obtain an audience with Count Florida Blanca. Disap-
pointed in this, he returned to Lisbon, leaving the conduct
of whatever questions might arise in the hands of Carmichael.

"As the business with which he is now charged requires
to be managed with uncommon address and delicacy, I
have advised him to seize some good occasion for obtaining
a particular audience to explain our desires specifically, but
in the most discreet manner, with the reasons and motives
on which they are founded. And I have told him, that I
apprehended the sooner this could be done, the better it
would be; since the affairs of Europe, far from being settled,
may soon produce a crisis highly favorable to the promotion
of our interests; and since our western settlers cannot long
brook delay. Hitherto he had only found a casual opportunity (that is to say, immediately after my arrival) to sug-

gest to the minister, in general terms without abruptness, our sincere disposition to be connected with Spain, in the most liberal and friendly manner; and for this purpose the apparent expediency of making arrangements respecting the navigation of the Mississippi, before any ill adventures shall happen in that quarter." *

What occurred immediately after Humphreys' departure is described in a letter that Carmichael wrote to Jefferson, interesting not only in connection with this special mission, but also as showing the difficulties under which Carmichael was placed while in Spain.

MADRID, 24 January, 1791.

Sir: Colonel Humphreys delivered to me your letter of the 6th of August on the 18th of the last month; nothing could equal my astonishment in finding that I have been employing my time in a situation that has been for many years disagreeable, so little to my own credit or to the satisfaction of my own country.

The only method which I could take in the moment was to show to a man who justly merits the confidence placed in him, the pains I had taken for information, and how improbable it was that I should spend my time and even my own fortune to procure intelligence without transmitting the materials which I obtained with great difficulty and considerable expense, that at least prove my zeal, tho' perhaps not my talents.

The next object will be to forward copies of all the dispatches which I find by your letter have not reached the Department. I cannot account for the detention of my letters. I know that I have had powerful enemies here, who from personal motives have in many instances endeavored to injure me.

I discovered that a servant who had lived with me more

---

* *Humphreys to the Secretary of State*, Lisbon, 6 February, 1791.

than six years had received money to a considerable amount from one of these persons, the C.t Cabarras. He has paid, and is paying, dearly the suborning my domestics, yet more from his own imprudence than my efforts.

On the 26th of February, I gave an account of a friendly conversation which I had with the C.te de Florida Blanca on that subject, which terminated to our mutual satisfaction.

The President will have probably communicated to you the letter I had the honor to write him on the first notice of his nomination : Least that letter should not have met with better fortune than so many others have done, I inclose a copy, as also one I wrote from Aranjuez on being advised by you that he had been pleased to continue me in my present employment.

You will see that I have no interested motive to influence my conduct ; I can say with truth that I have now to begin life (so far as the expression may be applied to independence and domestic ease), and I thought I could have done it with pleasure, until I received your letters by Colonel Humphreys.

I announced to the Department of Foreign Affairs the time and the manner in which I received the cyphers sent me. Colonel Humphreys has seen by the covers of those cyphers, and by certificates I took from persons who were present, or who delivered them, that it would have been highly imprudent in me to have made use of them. If they have ever been employed, no letter in cypher has ever reached me.

I sent duplicates of these certificates immediately to the department, and I find that by the list which you send me of letters received that these have not come to hand.

You will pardon this detail. It is necessary for my own tranquillity, which has suffered more than I can express for several years past, and more particularly since I have received your last letter. If my letters since the 26th of February have reached you, you will be convinced that no one here in the diplomatic line was so early or better informed

than I have been with respect to the apparent rupture between this country and Great Britain. I knew how it
would end, because I knew that measures begun in folly
would terminate in humiliation, and humiliation might lead
to something more.

Something however might have been done in a moment
of projects and apprehension, had not a certain negotiation
carried on our part at London transpired, and which I think
was known here rather from British policy than from the
vigilance of the Marquis del Campo. Entirely unacquainted
with this manœuvre, although in correspondence with the
person employed, I was suspected to be in the secret.
This suspicion banished confidence, which returns by slow
degrees. This circumstance induced me to stop entirely
my correspondence with G. M.; to continue it would have
done harm, and certainly could do no good.

I have seen extracts from the President's letter communicated to the Duke of Leeds, perhaps mutilated or forged,
to serve here the views of the British Cabinet : I do not yet
dispair of obtaining copies of those letters thro' the same
channel that I procured the first account of the demands of
G. B., and the signature of the late convention.

You will easily conceive that I must now discretionally
obey (from the change of circumstances) the latter part of
the instructions given me ; but, sir, the opportunities of
seeing the minister in the character I hold, are so rare, that
·there is little room for information (?). However active,
however punctual, I may be, I must wait until every ambassador, every minister, even if there was one from the Republic of Ragusa, have had their audience, before I can obtain
mine. You will see by the enclosed paper No. 1,* the conversation I have had with the minister. I have endeavored
indirectly to suggest ideas of the necessity of a speedy
determination in this government to adopt the measures
pointed out by your last letters. These suggestions have
been made to persons who have *now*, and probably will

---

*Missing.

have in future, much influence in the Cabinet, if the Queen lives. I shall communicate to you the effects which my representations may produce, and with Colonel Humphrey's advice and approbation. If occasion offers, and circumstances permit, I shall decidedly press the business.

This government is weak; the ministry is in a ticklish situation; the Queen governs, and governs with caprice; the people begin to dispute their sovereigns; and altho' they have no chiefs to look up to, the dissatisfaction is general. . . .

There is probably something in agitation here with respect to the affairs of the north. I shall endeavor to develop this business. Here they hold themselves in readiness to arm. The object is doubtful and unaccountable. It is a mixture of haughtiness and timidity. In fact, after having blundered into humiliation abroad, they want to appear respectable at home. This is an observation made to me by the Cͭ de Campomanes, Governor of the Council of Castile, who is, with those he can influence, decidedly of opinion that it is the interest of his country to form liberal and lasting connections with the United States. . . . *

WM. CARMICHAEL.

Gouverneur Morris had been authorized in October, 1789, to confer with the British ministers in order to learn their sentiments on the matters of controversy pending between the United States and Great Britain, and arising mainly from the treaty of 1783—that is, the detention of the western posts by England, the question of indemnification for negroes carried off contrary to treaty, a commercial treaty, and an exchange of ministers between the two powers. Morris had reported in substance that the ministers " equivocate on every proposal of a treaty of commerce, and authorize in their communications with Mr. Morris the same conclusions

---

*This letter was received by Jefferson, March 31st.

which have been drawn from those they had had from time to time with M⯑ Adams, and those through Maj⯑ Beckwith :* to wit, that they do not mean to submit their present advantages in commerce to the risk which might attend a discussion of them, whereon some reciprocity could not fail to be demanded—unless indeed we would agree to make it a treaty of *alliance*, as well as of *commerce*, so as to undermine our obligations with France. This mode of stripping that rival nation of its alliances they tried successfully with Holland, endeavored at with Spain, and have plainly and repeatedly suggested to us. For this they would probably relax some of the rigours they exercise against our commerce. That as to a minister, their Secretary for Foreign Affairs is disposed to exchange one, but meets with opposition in his cabinet, so as to render the issue uncertain."† Hence Jefferson concluded "that it would be dishonorable to the U. S., useless, even injurious, to renew the propositions for a treaty of commerce, or for the exchange of a minister: and that these subjects should now remain dormant, till they shall be brought forward earnestly by them."‡ The President reported to the Senate, 14 February, 1791, that from these conferences of Morris, he did "not infer any disposition on their part to enter into any arrangements merely commercial

---

* Major, afterwards Sir George Beckwith, had served in the British army through the Revolution, aud from 1787 to 1791, when there was no British minister accredited to the United States, he was entrusted with "an important and confidential mission," acting, in fact, as an unrecognized diplomatic agent. It was for his services in the West Indies that he was knighted.

† Jefferson's summary of Morris's letters.

‡ Jefferson's report to the President, 15 December, 1790.

4

. . . unless it could be extended to a treaty of alliance, offensive and defensive, or unless in the event of a rupture with Spain."

Here ended the episode. It may be remembered that in July, 1797, William Blount was expelled from the Senate for being concerned in a conspiracy to deliver New Orleans into the hands of the British, and for having instigated the Creeks and Cherokees to assist the British to conquer Louisiana.

WORTHINGTON CHAUNCEY FORD.

Washington. August, 1890.

UNITED STATES, 27 August, 1790.

Provided the dispute between Great Britain and Spain should come to the decision of arms, from a variety of circumstances (individually unimportant and inconclusive, but very much the reverse when compared and combined), there is no doubt in my mind that New Orleans and the Spanish ports above it on the Mississippi, will be among the first attempts of the former, and that the reduction of them will be undertaken by a combined operation from Detroit.

The *consequences* of having so formidable and enterprising a people as the British on both our flanks and rear, with their navy in front, as they respect our western settlements which may be seduced thereby, as they regard the security of the Union and its commerce with the West Indies, are too obvious to need enumeration.

What then should be the answer of the Executive of the United States to Ld Dorchester, in case he should apply for permission to march troops through the territory of the U.^{d} States from Detroit to the Mississippi?

What notice ought to be taken of the measure, if it

(43)

should be undertaken without leave, which is the most
probable proceeding of the two ? *

---

* August 27, 1890, Washington placed on paper these questions,
and sent them to the Vice-President, the members of his Cabinet, and
the Chief Justice, requesting their opinion in writing. A distinction,
perhaps of no importance, was made in the manner of asking these
gentlemen; for the opinion of the members of the Cabinet was " requested to be given," but " Mr. Jay will oblige the President of the
United States by giving his opinion." As to the form used with Mr.
Adams, no record appears.

REPLY OF THE VICE-PRESIDENT.

NEW YORK, 29 August, 1790.

SIR: That New Orleans, and the Spanish ports on the Mississippi, will be among the first attempts of the English, in case of a war with Spain, appears very probable : and that a combined operation from Detroit would be convenient to that end cannot be doubted.

The consequences on the western settlements, on the commerce with the West Indies, and on the general security and tranquillity of the American confederation, of having them in our rear, and on both our flanks, with their navy in front, are very obvious.

The interest of the United States duly weighed, and their duty conscientiously considered, point out to them, in the case of such a war, a neutrality, as long as it may be practicable. The people of these States would not willingly support a war, and the present government has not strength to command, nor enough of the general confidence of the nation to draw the men or money necessary, until the grounds, causes and necessity of it should become generally known, and universally approved. A pacific character, in opposition to a war-like temper, a spirit of conquest, or a disposition to military enterprise, is of great importance to us as to preserve in Europe: and therefore, we should not engage even in defensive war, until the

(45)

necessity of it should become apparent, or at least until we have it in our power to make it manifest, in Europe as well as at home.

In order to preserve an honest neutrality, or even the reputation of a disposition to it, the United States must avoid as much as possible every real wrong, and even every appearance of injury to either party. To grant to Lord Dorchester, in case he should request it, permission to march troops through the territory of the United States, from Detroit to the Mississippi, would not only have an appearance offensive to the Spaniards, of partiality to the English, but would be a real injury to Spain. The answer therefore to his lordship should be a refusal, in terms clear and decided, but guarded and dignified, in a manner which no Power has more at command than the President of the United States.

If a measure so daring, offensive and hostile as the march of troops through our territory to attack a friend, should be hazarded by the English, without leave, or especially after a refusal, it is not so easy to answer the question, what notice ought to be taken of it.

The Situation of our Country is not like that of the nations in Europe. They have generally large numbers of inhabitants in narrow territories: we have small numbers scattered over vast regions. The country through which the Brittons must pass from Detroit to the Mississippi, is, I suppose, so thinly inhabited, and at such a distance from all the populous settlements, that it would be impossible for the President of the United States to collect militia or march troops sufficient to resist the enterprise. After the step shall have been taken there are two ways for us to proceed : one is war, and the other negotiation. Spain would probably remonstrate to the President of the United States, but whether she should or not, the President of the United States should remonstrate to the King of Great Britain. It would not be expected I suppose, by our friends or enemies, that the United States should declare war at once. Nations are not obliged to declare war for every injury or even hostility. A tacit acquiescence under such an outrage, would be misinterpreted on all hands; by Spain as inimical to her, and by Britain as the effect of weakness, disunion and pusillanimity. Negotiation then is the only other alternative.

Negotiation in the present state of things is attended with peculiar difficulties. As the King of Great Britain twice proposed to the United States an exchange of ministers, once through M^r. Hartley and once through the Duke of Dorsett, and when the United States agreed to the proposition, flew from it : to send a minister again to St. James's till that Court explicitly promises to . send one to America, is an humiliation to which the United States ought never to submit. A remonstrance from sovereign to sovereign cannot be sent, but by an ambassador of some order or other : from minister of state to minister of state, it might be transmitted in many other ways : a remonstrance in the form of a letter from the American Minister of State to the Duke of Leeds, or whoever may be Secretary of State for Foreign Affairs, might be transmitted, through an envoy, minister plenipotentiary, or ambassador of the President of the United States, at Paris, Madrid or the Hague, and through the British ambassador at either of these courts. The utmost length that can now be gone with dignity, would be to send a minister to the Court of London, with instructions to present his credentials, demand an audience, make his remonstrance, but to make no establishment, and demand his audience of leave and quit the kingdom in one, two or three months, if a minister of equal degree were not appointed and actually sent to the President of the United States from the King of Great Britain.

It is a misfortune that in these critical moments and circumstances, the United States have not a minister of large views, mature age, information and judgment, and strict integrity, at the Courts of France, Spain, London and the Hague. Early and authentic intelligence from those courts may be of more importance than the expense; but as the representatives of the people, as well as the legislatures, are of a different opinion, they have made a very scanty provision for but a part of such a system. As it is, God knows where the men are to be found who are qualified for such missions and would undertake them. By an experience of ten years, which made me too unhappy at the time to be ever forgotten, I know that every artifice which can deceive, every temptation which can operate on hope or fear, ambition or avarice, pride or vanity, the love of society, pleasure or amusement, will be employed to divert and warp them from the true line of their duty and the impartial honour and interest of their country.

To the superior lights and information derived from office ; the more serene temper and profound judgment of the President of the United States, these crude and hasty thoughts concerning the points proposed, are humbly submitted, with every sentiment of respect and sincere attachment, by his most obedient and most humble servant,

JOHN ADAMS.

The President of the United States.

NEW YORK, 28 August, 1790.

SIR: The Case which I had yesterday the Honor of receiving from you, gave occasion to the following Remarks and Reflections.

Whether the Issue of the Negociations depending between the British and Spanish courts is Peace or War, it certainly is prudent to anticipate and be prepared for the consequences of either event. In the present state of things it would doubtless militate against the interests of the U. S., that the Spanish territories in question should be reduced, and remain under the Government of his B. majesty; and probably that circumstance would strongly unite with those others which must naturally lead him to regard the Possession of these Countries as a desirable Object.

If Permission to march Troops for that Purpose, thro' the territories of the U. S., should be requested. it will be necessary to consider

1. Whether the Laws of Nations entitle a *belligerent* power to a free Passage for Troops thro' the Territories of a *neutral* Nation? and

2, In Case the Right to such Passage be not a *perfect* one, whether circumstances render a Refusal or a compliance, most adviseable on the present occasion? .

(50)

The Right of Dominion involves that of the excluding (under the Restrictions imposed by Humanity) all Foreigners. This Right is very rigidly exercised by some States, particularly the Empire of China. European Nations consider this as a general Right or Rule, and as subject to Exceptions in favor not only of nations at *Peace*, but also of Nations at *War*. The exceptions with respect to the *former* do not touch the present question. Those which relate to the *latter*, seem to be comprized within *two* Classes, viz! cases of *urgent necessity*, and cases of *Convenience*. The present case belongs to the latter. Vattel, who well understood the subject, says in the 7th chapter of his 3d Book.—

That an *innocent* Passage is due to all Nations with whom a State is at Peace, and that this comprehends Troops equally with Individuals. That the Sovereign of the Country is to judge whether this Passage be *innocent*—that his Permission must be asked—and that an Entry into his Territories without his Consent, is a violation of the Rights of Dominion—that if the neutral Sovereign has *good* Reasons for refusing a Passage, he is not bound to grant it ;—but that if his Refusal is evidently unjust (the Passage requested being *unquestionably innocent*) a nation may do itself Justice, and take by Force, what it was unjustly denied—so that such Requests may be refused in all cases, except in those rare Instances, where it may be most evidently shown that the Passage required is absolutely without Danger or Inconvenience.

If the Passage in contemplation should appear to be of this Complection, a Refusal would generally be deemed improper, unless the United States should declare and make it an invariable maxim in their Policy, *never to permit the Troops of any Nation to pass thro' their country.* Such a measure *might* be wise, in case the the U. S. were in capacity to act accordingly; but that not being as yet the Case, it would perhaps in the present moment be unreasonable.

I say " such a measure *might* be wise "—whether it would or not, is a question that involves others, both legal and political, of great magnitude. Nations have *perfect* Rights. Regard to mutual Convenience may and often does induce Relaxations in the Exercise of them ; and those Relaxations, from Time and Usage, gradually assume to a certain Degree the Nature of Rights. I think it would appear on a full investigation of the Subject, that the United States being a new Nation, are not bound to yield the same Relaxations, which in Europe from long Practice and Acquiescence amount almost to an implied Cession ; and therefore, that they may justly exercise rigorously the Right of denying free Passage to foreign Troops. It is also to be observed, that if they deny this Priviledge to others, it will also be denied to them ; but this leads to political consequences and Considerations not necessary now to develop or investigate.

If a Passage should be requested and insisted upon, on the Ground of its being perfectly *innocent,* and accompanied with such Terms and Precautions, as that a Refusal, altho' justifiable, would not appear to be more than barely so; then it will be advisable to calculate the Probability of their being restrained by such a Refusal.

If the Probability should be, that they would nevertheless proceed; then it would become important to consider whether it would not be better to grant Permission, than by a Refusal to hazard one of two enevitable Inconveniences, viz.ᵗ that of opposing their Progress by Force of arms, and thereby risque being involved in the war; or of submitting to the Disgrace and Humiliation of permitting them to proceed with impunity. In my opinion it would in such a Case be most prudent, considering the actual state of our affairs, to consent to the Passage. The answer therefore to be given to Lord Dorchester, in Case he should apply for Permission to march Troops thro' the Territory of the U. S. from Detroit to the Mississippi, will I think necessarily depend on the nature of the Propositions contained in the application, compared with the beforementioned Principles and Probabilities.

As to the notice proper to be taken of the measure, if it should be undertaken *without* leave? There appears to me to be no choice. Such a measure would then be so manifest a Departure from the usage of civilized Nations, so flagrant and wanton a violation of the Rights of Sovereignty, and so strong and indecent a Mark of Disrespect and Defiance, that their march (if after Prohibition persisted in) should I think be opposed and prevented at every Risque and Hazard.

But these Remarks in my Judgment retain but little Force when applied to the leading of Troops from Posts in their actual Possession, thro' Territories under their actual Jurisdiction, altho' both the Posts and the Territories of right belong to the U. S. If therefore they should march Troops from such posts, thro' such Territories, that measure would not appear to me to afford *particular* cause of complaint. On their arrival by such a Route at the Mississippi, they may in virtue of the 8th Article of the Treaty navigate it up to its source, or down to the ocean.

This Subject naturally brings into view a question both difficult and important, viz! whether as the Possession of the Floridas would afford G. Britain additional Means and Facilities of annoying the U. S. the latter would for that Reason be justifiable in endeavoring to prevent it by direct and hostile opposition? The Danger of permitting any Nation so to preponderate, as to endanger the security of others, introduced into the Politics the Idea of preserving a Ballance of Power. How far the Principles which have thence been inferred, are applicable to the present Case, would merit serious Inquiry, if the U. S. had only to consider what might be right and just on the occasion; but as the state of their affairs strongly recommends Peace, and as there is much Reason to presume that it would be more prudent for them *at present* to permit Britain to conquer and hold the Floridas, than engage in a War to prevent it, such Inquiries would be premature.

With the most perfect Respect and Esteem I have the Honor to be, Sir,

Your most obt. and most humble servant,

JOHN JAY.

The President of the United States.

Opinion on the Questions stated in the President's note of August 27, 1790.

I am so deeply impressed with the magnitude of the dangers which will attend our government if Louisiana and the Floridas be added to the British Empire, that in my opinion we ought to make ourselves parties in the *general war* expected to take place, should this be the only means of preventing the calamity.

But I think we should defer this step as long as possible; because war is full of chances which may relieve us from the necessity of interfering; and if necessary, still the later we interfere the better we shall be prepared.

It is often indeed more easy to prevent the capture of a place, than to retake it. Should it be so in the case in question, the difference between the two operations of preventing and retaking, will not be so costly as two, three, or four years more of war.

So that I am for preserving neutrality as long, and entering into the war as late, as possible.

If this be the best course, it decides in a good degree what should be our conduct if the British ask leave to march troops thro' our territory, or march them without leave.

It is well enough agreed in the Law of Nations, that

for a Neutral power to give or refuse permission to the troops of either belligerent party to pass through their territory, is no breach of neutrality, provided the same refusal or permission be extended to the other party.

If we give leave of passage then to the British troops, Spain will have no just cause of complaint against us, provided we extend the same leave to her when demanded.

If we refuse (as indeed we have a right to do), and the troops should pass notwithstanding, of which there can be little doubt, we shall stand committed. For either we must enter immediately into the war, or pocket an acknowledged insult in the face of the world; and one insult pocketed soon produces another.

There is indeed a middle course, which I should be inclined to prefer, that is, to avoid giving any answer. They will proceed notwithstanding. But to do this under our silence, will admit of palliation and produce apologies from military necessity; and will leave us free to pass it over without dishonor, or to make it a handle of quarrel hereafter, if we should have use for it as such. But if we are obliged to give an answer, I think the occasion not such as should induce us to hazard that answer which might commit us to the war at so early a stage of it; and therefore that the passage should be permitted.

If they should pass without having asked leave, I

5

should be for expressing our dissatisfaction to the British court, and keeping alive an altercation on the subject, till events should decide whether it is most expedient to accept their apologies, or profit of the aggression as a cause of war.

Th: Jefferson.

August 28, 1790.

2 August, 1790.

We have a right to the Navig'n of the Missi.

    1. by Nature.

    2. by Treaty.

It is *necessary* to us

    More than half the territory of the U. S. is on the
waters of that river.

    200,000 of their citizens are seated on them.

    These have no other outlet for their tob?, rice, corn,
hemp, lumber, house-timber, ship-timber, etc.

We have hitherto borne the indecision of Spain, Because
we wish peace.

    because our Western citizens have had vent at home
for their productions.

A surplus of production begins now to demand foreign
markets.

Whenever they shall say 'We cannot, we will not, be
longer shut up,' the U. S. will soon be reduced to the
following dilemma :

    1. to force them to acquiescence.

    2. to separate from them, rather than take part in a
war against Spain.

    3. or to preserve them in our Union, by joining them
in the war.

The 1st is neither in our principles nor our power.

2. A multitude of reasons decide against the 2d.

    One only shall be spoken out : the Nation that gives

(59)

up half its territory, rather than engage in a just war
to preserve it, will not keep the other half long.

3. the third is the only alternative we must necessarily
adopt.

How are we to obtain that navigation?

   A. By Force.

      I. Acting separately.

         that we can Effect this with certainty and prompt-
itude all circumstances decide.

Obj. We cannot retain N. Orleans, for instance, were we
to take it.

Ans. A moderate force may be so secured so as to hold
out till succoured.   Our succours can be prompt and
effectual.

Suppose after taking it, we withdraw our force.

     If Spain retakes it by an expedition, we can recover
it by a counter-exped'n, and so, as often as the case
shall happen.

     Their expeditions will be slow, expensive, and lead
to catastrophe.   Ours sudden, economical, and a
check can have no consequences.

We should associate the country to our union, the inhabitants wish this.

     they are not disposed to be of the Spanish govern-
ment.

It is idle in Spain to suppose our Western habitants will
submit to their gov'm't.

     they could be quiet but a short time under a gov'm't
so repugnant to their feelings.   Were they to come
under it for present purposes, it w^d be with a view
to throw it off soon.   Should they remain they would

communicate a spirit of independence to those with whom they should be mixed.

II. Acting in conjunction with Gr. Br. with a view to partition, the Floridas (includs N. Orleans) would be assigned to us.

Louisiana (or all the country on the West? waters of yᵉ Missi.) to them.

We confess that such an Alliance is not what we would wish ;

because it may eventually lead us into embarrassing . situations as to our best friend, and put the power of two n'bors into yᵉ hands of one.

L.ᵈ Lansdowne has declared he gave the Floridas to Spain rather than to the U. S. as a bone of discord with the H. of Bourbon, and of reunion with Gr. Br. Connolly's attempt* (as well as other facts) proves they keep it in view.

B. By Negociation.

I. What must Spain do of *necessity* ?

The conduct of Spain has proved the occlusion of the Missi. is system with her ; if she opens it now, it will be because forced by imperious circumstances. She will consequently shut it again when these circumstances cease.

Treaty will be no obstacle.

irregularities, real and pretended, in our navigators, will furnish colour enough, perpetual broils, and finally war will ensue.

---

* On this mission of Connolly see Gayarre, *History of Louisiana under the Spanish Domination*, 235, and Brown, *Political Beginnings of Kentucky*, 182 ,—one of the publications of the Filson Club, and of great value.

prudence, and even necessity, imposes on us the law of settling the matter now, *finally*, and not by *halves*. With experience of the past, and prospect of the future, it w^d be imbecility in us to accept ye naked navigation. With that, we must have what will secure its continuance : that is, a port near the mouth, to receive our vessels, and protect the navigation.

But even this will not secure the Floridas and Louisiana against Gr. Brit.

if we are neutral, she will wrest those possessions from Spain.

the inhabitants (French, English, Scotch, Americans) would prefer Engl^d to Spain.

II. What then had Spain better do of *choice?*

Cede to us all territory on our side the Mississippi.

on condition that we guarantee all her poss'n on the western waters of that river, she agreeing further to subsidize us, if the guarantee brings us into the war.

Should Gr. Br. possess herself of the Floridas and Louisiana, her governing principles are Conquest, Colonization, Commerce, Monopoly.

She will establish powerful colonies in them.

these can be poured into the gulph of Mexico, for any sudden enterprise there.

or invade Mexico their next neighbor by land; whilst a fleet co-operates along shore, and cuts off relief.

and proceed successively from colony to colony.

With respect to us, if Gr. Br. establishes herself on our whole land board, our lot will be bloody and eternal war

or indissoluble confederacy.

Which ought we to choose?

What will be the lot of the Span. colonies in the jaws of such a confederacy?

What will secure the Ocean against Monopoly?

Safer for Spain that we should be her neighbor, than England.

Conquest not in our principles: inconsistent with our govm't.

Not our interest to cross the Mississippi for ages,

And will never be our interest to remain united with those who do.

Intermediate chances save the trouble of calculating so far forward.

Consequences of this cession, and guarantee.

1. Every subject of difference will be removed from between Spain and the U. S.

2. Our interest w^{ll} be strongly engaged in her retaining her American possessions.

3. Spain will be quieted as to Louisiana and her territories west of that.

4. She may employ her whole force in defence of her islands and Southern possessions.

5. If we preserve our neutrality, it will be a very partial one to her.

6. If we are forced into the war, it will be, as we wish, on the side of the H. of Bourbon.

7. Our privateers will commit formidable depred'n on ye Brit. trade, and occupy much of their force.

8. By withold'g supplies of provision, as well as by·

concurring in exped'ns, y? Brit isl?ˢ will be in im-
minent danger.

9. Their expences of precaution, both for their continental and insular poss'ns will be so augmented,
as to give a hope of running their credit down.

In fine, for a narrow strip of barren, detached,
and expensive country, Spain secures the rest of
her territory, and makes an ally where she might
have a dangerous enemy.*

---

* These heads are in Jefferson's *MS.*, but differ somewhat from those
printed in his *Works*, ix, 412.

HEADS OF CONSIDERATION ON THE CONDUCT WE ARE TO OBSERVE IN THE WAR BETWEEN SPAIN AND GR. BRITAIN, AND PARTICULARLY SHOULD THE LATTER ATTEMPT THE CONQUEST OF LOUISIANA AND THE FLORIDAS.

[12 July, 1790.]

The danger to us sh^d G. B. possess herself of Louisiana and the Floridas.

Beyond the Missi. a territory equal to half ours.

She would seduce our Cis-Missi. possessions.

Because N. Orleans will draw to it the dependence of all those waters.

By her language, laws, religion, manners, govent, commerce, capitals.

By the markets she can offer them in the gulph of Mexico.

She would then have a territory the double of ours.

She would take away the markets of the Atlantic States,

By furnishing the same articles cheaper, tob?, rice, indigo, bread, lumber, fur.

She would encircle us completely, her possessions forming a line on our land boards, her fleets on our sea board. Instead of two neighbors balancing each other, we should have one with ye strength of both.

Would the prevention of this be worth a War?

Consider our abilities to make a war.

Our operations would be by land only.

How many men would it need to employ?—their cost?

Our resources by taxation and credit equal to this.

Weigh the evil of this new accumulation of debt.

Against the loss of market and eternal danger and expence of such a neighbor.

But no need to take a part as yet. We may choose our own time for that.

Delay gives us many chances to avoid it altogether.

They may not single out that object.

They may fail in it.

France and Spain may recover it.

The difference between preventing and retaking, overbal^ed by benefits of delay.

Enables us to be better prepared.

To stipulate with Spain and France advantages for our assistance.

Suppose these our ultimate views, what is to be done at this time?

1. As to Spain.

If she be as sensible as we are, that she cannot save Louisiana and the Floridas, might she not prefer their Independ^ce to their Subject^n to Gr. Br.?

Can we not take advantage of C^t D'Estaing's propos'n to communicate thro' the court of France our ideas on this subject and our readiness to join them in guarantee?

This might save us from a war, if Gr. Br. respects our weight in a war. If she does not, it would place the war on popular ground.

2. As to England, say to B.[eckwith] :—

That as to a treaty of commerce we h^d never desired it but on terms of perfect reciprocity.

That therefore we never thought to give any price for it but itself.

That we had wished for it to avoid giving mutual bounds to the commerce of both nations.

But that we have the measures in our own power which may save us from loss.

That as to the alliance they propose, it would involve us against France and Spain.

And considered even in a moral view, no price could repay such an abandonm! of character.

That we are truly disposed to remain strictly neutral. Tho' we must confess y! we sh! view in a very serious light attempts to extend themselves along our frontier, and destroy all balance in our neighborhood.

[The latter sentiment it might be advantageous to express, because if there be any difference of op'n in her councils whether to bend their force ag! North or South America (and certainly there is room for difference) and if these operations be nearly balanced, the possibility of drawing an enemy the more on themselves, might determine the balance.]*

* A single sheet in Jefferson's *MS.*, undated and without signature. It is the first draft of a paper drawn up by Jefferson as the basis of a reply to the mission of George Beckwith, some particulars of which are given in a note to the opinion of Hamilton, in the pages following. The paper as completed is printed, with errors, in the *Works of Jefferson*, ix, 409, and differs in many details from this draft.

New-York, Sept. 15, 1790.

The urgent avocations in which I have been engaged, towards putting in a train of execution the laws of the last session affecting my department, and a desire of reflecting maturely, and giving the reasons for the result of my reflections fully, have caused me to delay longer than I wished the answer to the questions with which you honored me, and I hope will excuse the delay.

The judgments formed, in particular cases, are almost always connected with a general train of ideas in respect to some more comprehensive principles or relations; and I had thought it advisable to lay that train before you, for the better explanation of the grounds of the opinions I now give, or may hereafter have occasion to give, on the like subjects, in obedience to your commands.

I feel no small regret in troubling you with the perusal of so voluminous a discussion; but as I thought it would be satisfactory to you to have the reasons of the opinions you required fully submitted to your consideration, I conceived it to be more consistent with my duty to risk some intrusion on your time, than to withhold any consideration that appeared to me of weight enough to enter into the determination.

The President of the United States.

NEW-YORK, Sept. 15, 1790.

Answer to Questions proposed by the President of the United States to the Secretary of the Treasury.

QUESTION THE FIRST.—"What should be the answer of the Executive of the United States to Lord Dorchester, in case he should apply for permission to march troops through the territory of said States, from Detroit to the Mississippi?"

ANSWER.—In order to a right judgment of what ought to be done in such case, it may be of use previously to consider the following points:

First.—Whether there be a right to *refuse* or *consent*, as shall be thought most for the interest of the United States.

Secondly.—The consequences to be expected from *refusal* or *consent.*

Thirdly.—The motives to the one or to the other.

As to the first point, if it were to be determined upon principle only, without regard to precedents or opinions, there would seem to be no room for hesitation about the right to refuse. The exclusive jurisdiction which every independent nation has over its own territory, appears to involve in it the right of prohibiting to all others the use of that territory in any way disagreeable to itself, and more especially for any

(69)

purpose of war, which always implies a degree of danger and inconvenience, with the exception only of cases of necessity.

And if the United States were in a condition to do it without material hazard, there would be strong inducements to their adopting it as a general rule never to grant a passage for a voluntary expedition of one power against another, unless obliged to it by treaty.

But the present situation of the United States is too little favorable to encountering hazards, to authorize attempts to establish rules, however eligible in themselves, which are repugnant to the received maxims or usages of nations.

It is therefore necessary to inquire what those maxims or usages enjoin in the case suggested.

With regard to usage, it has been far from uniform. There are various instances in ancient and modern times of similar permissions being demanded—many, in which they have been granted; others in which they have been refused, and the refusal acquiesced in; but perhaps more in which, when refused, a passage has been forced, and the doing of it has often been deemed justifiable.

Opinions are not more harmonious. Among those who may be considered as authorities on such subjects, Puffendorf and Barbeyrac confine within narrow limits *the right of passage* through neutral territories; while Grotius and Vattel, particularly the former, allow to it greater latitude. Puffendorf treats it not as a natural right, but as derived from compact or concession; especially when the enemy of a neighboring state desires leave to march troops through a neutral country against its neighbor. For it seems (says he) to be a part of *the duty which we owe to our neighbors*, especially such as have been kind and friendly, not to suffer any hostile power to march through our country to their prejudice, *provided we can hinder the design with no great inconvenience to ourselves.* And as it may have a tendency to make our own country the theatre of the war (since the power intended to be attacked may justifiably march within our limits to meet the approaching enemy), he concludes that it is the safest way of acting in such case, *if we can do it without any considerable prejudice to our own affairs*, to deny the enemy passage, and *actually to oppose him* if he endeavors to force it without our consent. But if we are either too weak to hinder his progress, or must on this score engage in a dangerous war, he admits that the plea of necessity will fairly justify us to our neighbor.

Examples, he adds, have little force on the decision of the question. For, generally, as people have been stronger or weaker, they have required passage with modesty or with confidence, and have in like manner granted or refused it to others.*

Barbeyrac, in his Commentary on Grotius, is still

---

* Puffendorf's Laws of Nature and Nations, pages 239, 240.

stronger against the right of passage.* He affirms
that, even though we have nothing to apprehend from
those who desire a passage, we are not therefore
obliged in rigor to grant it. It necessarily follows,
says he, from the right of property, that the proprietor
may refuse another the use of his goods. Humanity,
indeed, requires that he should grant that use to those
who stand in need of it, when it can be done without
any considerable inconvenience to himself; but if he
even then refuses it, though he transgresses his duty,
he does no wrong, properly so called, *except they are
in extreme necessity*, which is superior to all ordinary
rules. Thus far, and no further, extends the reserve
with which it is supposed the establishment of property is accompanied.

Grotius, on the other hand, expresses himself thus : †
A free passage ought to be granted to persons where
just occasion shall require, over any lands, or rivers,
or such parts of the sea as belong to any nation; and,
after enumerating several examples in support of his
position, he concludes that the *middle opinion* is best;
to wit, that the liberty of passing ought first to be demanded, and if denied, may be claimed by force.
Neither, says he, can it be reasonably objected that
there may be suspicion of danger from the passing of
a multitude; for one man's right is not diminished by

* Note 1 on Book II., Chap. III., § xiii.

† Rights of War and Peace, Book II., Chap. II., § xiii., Nos. 1, 2, 3, 4.

another man's fear. Nor is the fear of provoking that prince against whom he that desires to pass is engaged in a *just* war, a sufficient reason for refusing him passage. Nor is it any more an excuse that he may pass another way, for this is what every body may equally allege, and so this right by passing would be entirely destroyed. But it is enough that the passage be requested, without any fraud or ill design, by the nearest and most convenient way. *If*, indeed, he who desires to pass undertakes an *unjust* war, or if he brings people who are my enemies along with him, I *may* deny him a passage ; *for in this case* I have a right to meet and oppose him, even in his own land, and to intercept his march. Thus it would seem to be the opinion of Grotius, that a party engaged in a *just* war has a right, of course, to a passage through a neutral territory, which can scarcely, if at all, be denied him, even on the score of danger or inconvenience to the party required to grant it.

But Vattel, perhaps the most accurate and approved of the writers on the laws of nations, preserves a mean between these* different opinions. This is the sum of what he advances : That an *innocent passage* is *due* to all nations with whom a state is at peace, for troops equally with individuals, and to annoy as well as to avoid an enemy. That the party asking and the party asked are both, in different degrees, judges of

---

* Book III., Chap. VII., §§ 119, 120, 121, 122, 123.

6

the question *when innocent?* That where the party asked has *good reasons* for refusing, he is not under any obligation to grant, and in *doubtful* cases his judgment *ought to be definitive;* but in evident ones, or those in which the harmlessness of the passage is manifest, the party asking may, in the last resort, judge for himself, and after *demand* and *refusal* may force his way. That nevertheless, as it is very difficult for the passage of a powerful army to be absolutely innocent, and still more difficult for its innocence to be apparent, a refusal ought to be submitted to, *except* in those *very rare* cases when it can be shown in the most palpable manner that the passage required is absolutely without danger or inconvenience. And lastly, that this right of passage is only *due* in a war *not materially unjust.*

Perhaps the only inference to be drawn from all this is, that there exists in the practice of nations and the dogmas of political writers a certain vague pretension to a right of passage in particular cases, and according to circumstances, which is sufficient to afford to the strong a pretext for claiming and exercising it when it suits their interests, and to render it always dangerous to the weak to refuse, and sometimes not less so to grant it.

It is, nevertheless, a proper inquiry, whether a refusal could be placed on such ground as would give a reasonable cause of umbrage to the party refused, and as in the eye of the world would justify it.

Against the propriety of a refusal are the following circumstances: That there is no connection between us and Spain, which obliges us to it. That the passage asked will be down rivers, and for the most part through an uninhabited wilderness, whence no injury to our citizens or settlements will be apprehended: and that the number of troops to be marched, especially considering the route, will probably not be such, as on their own account, to be a serious cause of alarm. These circumstances may give our refusal the complexion of partiality to Spain, and of indisposition towards Britain, which may be represented as a deviation from the spirit of exact neutrality.

In support of the propriety of a refusal, the following is the only assignable reason; that it is safer for us to have two powerful, but *rival* nations, bordering upon our two extremities, than to have one powerful nation pressing us on both sides, and in capacity, hereafter, by posts and settlements, to envelop our whole interior frontier.

The good offices of Spain in the late war; the danger of the seduction of our western inhabitants; the probable consequences to the trade of the Atlantic States, are considerations rather to be contemplated as motives, than alleged as reasons.

The first reason, however, is of a nature to satisfy the mind of the justice of a refusal; admitting the authority of the more moderate opinions, which have been cited. And the danger, too, upon the supposition of which it is founded, appears to be obvious enough to vindicate it, in the opinion of the disinterested part of mankind; little likely as it may be to engage the acquiescence of the party whose wishes would be thwarted by the refusal. It deserves, notwithstanding, to be noticed on this point, that the ground of dissent would not result from the thing itself—that is, the *mere passage*—but from the nature of the *acquisition*, to which it would give facility. This circumstance may somewhat obscure the clearness of the conclusion, that there is a perfect right to refuse.

But upon the whole, there does not appear to be room enough for a scruple about the right, to deter from refusal, if upon examination it shall be found expedient.

Does the right of consenting to the passage stand upon ground equally unexceptionable?

This question Vattel answers in the following manner : * "When I have no reason to refuse the passage, the party against whom it is granted has *no room for complaint*, much less for making it a pretence for war; since I did no more than what the law of nations enjoins. Neither has he any right to require that I should deny the passage, because he is not to hinder me from doing what I think is agreeable to my duty, and *even* on occasion *when I might with justice deny*

---

* Vattel, Book III., Chap. vii., Section 127.

the passage, it is *allowable* in me *not to make use* of my right; *especially when I should be obliged to support my refusal by my sword.* Who will take upon him to complain of my having permitted the war to be carried into his own country, rather than draw it on myself? It cannot be expected that I should take up arms in his favor, unless obliged to it by a treaty." And Puffendorf admits, as has been before noted, that if we are either *too weak* to hinder his progress, or must on that score engage in a *dangerous* war, the plea of necessity will fairly justify us to our neighbor.

Nothing need be added to reasoning so perspicuous and convincing. It does not admit of a moment's doubt, as a general rule, that a neutral state, unfettered by any stipulation, is not bound to expose itself to a war, merely to shelter a neighbor from the approaches of its enemy. It remains to examine, if there are any circumstances, in our particular case, capable of forming an exception to that rule.

It is not to be forgotten that we received from France, in our late revolution, essential succor, and from Spain valuable countenance, and some direct aid. It is also to be remembered, that France is the intimate ally of Spain, and there subsists a connection by treaty between the former power and the United States.

It might thence be alleged that obligations of gratitude towards these powers require that we should run some risk, rather than concur in a thing prejudical to either of them, and particularly in favor of that very nation against which they assisted us. And the natural impulse of every good heart will second the proposition, till reason has taught it that refinements of this kind are to be indulged with caution in the affairs of nations.

Gratitude is a word, the very sound of which imposes something like respect. Where there is even an appearance upon which the claim to it can be founded, it can seldom be a pleasing task to dispute that claim. But where a word may become the basis of a political system, affecting the essential interests of the state, it is incumbent upon those who have any concern in the public administration, to appreciate its true import and application.

It is necessary, then, to reflect, however painful the reflection, that gratitude is a duty, a sentiment, which between nations can rarely have any solid foundation. Gratitude is only due to a kindness or service, the predominant object of which is the interest or benefit of the party to whom it is performed. Where the interest or benefit of the party performing is the predominant cause of it, however there may result a debt, in cases in which there is not an immediate adequate and reciprocal advantage, there can be no room for the sentiment of gratitude. Where there is such an advantage, there is then not even a debt. If the motive to the act, instead of being the benefit of the party to whom it is done, should be a compound of the interest of the party doing it and of detriment to some other, of whom he is the enemy and the rival, there is still less room for so noble and refined a sentiment. This analysis will serve as a test of our true situation, in regard both to France and Spain.

It is not to be doubted, that the part which the courts of France and Spain took in our quarrel with Great Britain, is to be attributed, not to an attachment to our independence or liberty, but to a desire of diminishing the power of Great Britain by severing the British Empire. This they considered as an interest of very great magnitude to them. In this their calculations and their passions conspired. For this, they united their arms with ours, and encountered the expenses and perils of war. This has been accomplished; the advantages of it are mutual; and so far the account is balanced.

In the progress of the war* they lent us money, as necessary to its success, and during our inability to pay they have forborne to press us for it. The money we ought to exert ourselves to repay with interest, and as well for the loan of it, as for the forbearance to urge the repayment of the sums which have become due, we ought always to be ready to make proportionate acknowledgments, and when opportunities shall offer, returns answerable to the nature of the service.

---

* France has made us one loan since the peace.

Let it be added to this, that the conduct of France in the manner of affording her aid, bore the marks of a liberal policy. She did not endeavor to extort from us, as the price of it, any disadvantageous or humiliating concessions. In this respect, however, she may have been influenced by an enlightened view of her own interest. She entitled herself to our esteem and good will. These dispositions towards her ought to be cherished and cultivated; but they are very distinct from a spirit of romantic gratitude, calling for sacrifices of our substantial interests. preferences inconsistent with sound policy, or complaisances incompatible with our safety.

The conduct of Spain towards us presents a picture far less favorable. The direct aid we received from her during the war was inconsiderable in itself, and still more inconsiderable compared with her faculty of aiding us. She refrained from acknowledging our independence; has never acceded to the treaty of commerce made with France, though a right of doing it was reserved to her, nor made any other treaty with us; she has maintained possessions within our acknowledged limits without our consent; she perseveringly obstructs our sharing in the navigation of the Mississippi, though it is a privilege essential to us, and to which we consider ourselves as having an indisputable title. And perhaps it might be added upon good ground, that she has not scrupled to intrigue with leading individuals in the western country, to seduce them from our interests, and to attach them to her own.

Spain therefore must be regarded, upon the whole, as having slender claims to peculiar good will from us. There is certainly nothing that authorizes her to expect we should expose ourselves to any extraordinary jeopardy for her sake. And to conceive that any considerations relative to France ought to be extended to her, would be to set up a doctrine altogether new in politics. The ally of our ally· has no claim, as such, to our friendship. We may have substantial grounds of dissatisfaction against him, and act in consequence of them, even to open hostility, without derogating in any degree from what we owe to our ally.

This is so true, that if a war should really ensue between Great Britain and Spain, and if the latter should persist in excluding us from the Mississippi (taking it for granted our claim to share in its navigation is well founded), there can be no reasonable ground of doubt that we should be at liberty, if we thought it our interest, consistently with our present engagements with France, to join Britain against Spain.

How far it might be expedient to place ourselves in a situation which, in case France should eventually become a party in the war, might entangle us in opposite duties on the score of the stipulated guarantee of her West India possessions, or might have a tendency to embroil us with her, would be a mere question of prudential and liberal calculation, which would have nothing to do with the right of taking side against Spain.

These are truths necessary to be contemplated with freedom, because it is impossible to foresee what events may spring up, or whither our interests may point; and it is very important to distinguish with accuracy how far we are bound, and where we are free.

However vague the obligations of gratitude may be between nations, those of good faith are precise and determinate. Within their true limits, they can hardly be held too sacred. But by exaggerating them, or giving them a fanciful extension, they would be in danger of losing their just force. This would be converting them into fetters, which a nation would ere long be impatient to break, as consistent neither with its prosperity nor its safety. Hence, while it is desirable to maintain with fidelity our engagements to France, it is advisable, on all occasions, to be aware that they oblige us to nothing towards Spain.

From this view of the subject, there does not appear any circumstance in our case capable of forming an exception to the general rule; and, as it is certain that there can hardly be a situation less adapted to war than that in which we now find ourselves, we can, with the greatest sincerity, offer the most satisfactory excuse to Spain for not withholding our consent, if our own interests do not decide us to a contrary course.

The conclusion from what has been said is, that there is a right either to refuse or consent, as shall be judged for the interest of the United States; though the right to consent is less questionable than the right to refuse.

The consequences to be expected from refusal or consent present themselves next to consideration. Those of consent shall be first examined.

An increase of the means of annoying us in the same hands is a certain ill consequence of the acquisition of the Floridas and Louisiana by the British. This will result not only from contiguity to a greater part of our territory, but from the increased facility of acquiring an undivided influence over all the Indian tribes inhabiting within the borders of the United States.

Additional danger of the dismemberment of the western country is another ill consequence to be apprehended from that acquisition. This will arise as well from the greater power of annoying us, as from the greater power which it is likely would be pursued by that nation, if in possession of the key to the only outlet for the productions of that country. Instead of shutting, they would probably open the door to its inhabitants, and by conciliating their good will on the one hand, and making them sensible on the other of their dependence on them for the continuance of so essential an advantage, they might hold out to them the most powerful temptation to a desertion of their connection with the rest of the United States. The avarice and ambition of individuals may be made to co-operate in favor of those views.

A third ill consequence of that acquisition would be, material injury, in time to come, to the commerce of the Atlantic States. By rendering New Orleans the emporium of the products of the western country, Britain would, at a period not *very* distant, have little occasion for supplies of provisions for their islands from the Atlantic States; and for their European market they would derive from the same source copious supplies of tobacco and other articles now furnished by the Southern States: whence a great diminution of the motives to establish liberal terms of commercial intercourse with the United States collectively.

These consequences are all expressed or implied in the form of the question stated by the President. And as far as our consent can be supposed likely to have influence upon the event, they constitute powerful objections to giving it.

If even it should be taken for granted that our consent or refusal would have no influence either way, it would not even then cease to be disagreeable to concur in a thing apparently so inauspicious to our interests. And it deserves attention, that our concurrency might expose us to the imputation either of want of foresight to discover a danger, or of vigor to withstand it.

But there is almost always in such cases a comparison of evils; and the point of prudence is, to make choice of that course which threatens the fewest or the least, or sometimes the least certain. The consequences of refusal are therefore to be weighed against those of consent.

It seems to be a matter taken for granted by the writers upon the subject, that a refusal ought to be accompanied with a resolution to support it, if necessary, by the sword ; or in other words, to oppose the passage, if attempted to be forced, or to resent the injury, if circumstances should not permit an effectual opposition. This, indeed, is implied in the nature of the thing; for to what purpose refuse, unless it be intended to make good the refusal? or how avoid disgrace, if our territories are suffered to be violated with impunity, after a formal and deliberate prohibition of passage?

There are cases in which a nation may, without ignominy, wink at an infraction of its rights; but this does not appear to be one of them. After having been asked its permission and having refused it, the presumption will be that it has estimated the consequences, calculated its means, and is prepared to assert and uphold its rights. If the contrary of this should turn out to be its conduct, it must bring itself into contempt for inviting insult which it is unable to repel, and manifesting ill-will towards a power which it durst not resist. As, on the one hand, there cannot be conceived to be a greater outrage than to pass through our country, in defiance of our *declared* disapprobation ; so, on the other, there cannot be a greater humiliation than to submit to it.

The consequence therefore of refusal, if not effectual, must be absolute disgrace or immediate war. This *appears*, at least, to be the alternative.

Whether a refusal would have the desired effect, is at best problematical. The presumption, perhaps, is, that Great Britain will have adverted to the possibility of it; and if, under the uncertainty of what would be our conduct, she should still have resolved on prosecuting the enterprise through our territory, that she will at the same time have resolved, either to ask no questions, or to disregard our dissent. It is not unlikely that the reasoning of the British cabinet will have been to this effect :—If the United States have no predilection for Spain, or if their views of their own interest are not opposed to the acquisition we meditate, they will not withhold their consent; if either the one or the other be the case, it ought to be determined beforehand, whether their enmity be a greater evil, than the projected acquisition a good; and if we do not choose to renounce the one, we must be prepared to meet the other.

A further ill consequence of the refusal, if ineffectual, not *wholly* destitute of weight, is this, that Great Britain would then think herself under less obligation to keep measures with us, and would feel herself more at liberty to employ every engine in her power to make her acquisition as prejudicial to us as possible ; whereas, if no impediment should be thrown in the way by us, more good humor may beget greater moderation, and, in the progress of things, concessions securing us may be made, as the price of our future neutrality. An explicit recognition of our right to navigate the Mississippi to and from the ocean, with the possession of New Orleans, would greatly mitigate the causes of apprehension from the conquest of the Floridas by the British.

The consequences of refusal or consent constitute leading motives to the one or to the other; which now claim a more particular discussion.

It has been seen that the ill effects to be apprehended from the conquest of the Spanish territories in our neighborhood are, an increase of the means whereby we may be hereafter annoyed, and of the danger of the separation of the western country from the rest of the Union; and a future interference with the trade of the Atlantic States, in a manner, too, not conducive to the general weal.

As far as there is a prospect that a refusal would be an impediment to the enterprise, the considerations which have been mentioned afford the strongest inducements to it. But if *that* effect of it be doubtful, the force of these inducements is proportionably diminished; if improbable, it nearly ceases. The prospect in this case would be, that a refusal would aggravate instead of preventing the evil it was intended to obviate. And it must be acknowledged that the success of it is, at least, *very doubtful*.

The consideration that our assent may be construed

into want of foresight or want of vigor, though not to be disregarded, would not be sufficient to justify our risking a war in our present situation. The cogent reasons we have to avoid a war are too obvious and intelligible, not to furnish an explanation of and an apology for our conduct in this respect.

Whatever may be the calculations with regard to the probable effect of a refusal, it ought to be predicated upon the supposition that it may not be regarded, and accompanied with a determination to act as a proper attention to national dignity would in such an event dictate. This would be to make war.

For it is a *sound maxim*, that a state had better hazard any calamities than submit tamely to absolute disgrace.

Now it is manifest, that a government scarcely ever had stronger motives to avoid war, than that of the United States at the present juncture. They have much to dread from war; much to expect from peace; something to hope from negotiation, in case of a rupture between Britain and Spain.

We are but just recovering from the effects of a long, arduous, and exhausting war. The people but just begin to realize the sweets of repose. We are vulnerable both by water and land; without either fleet or army. We have a considerable debt in proportion to the resources which the state of things permits the government to command. Measures have been recently entered upon for the restoration of credit, which a war could hardly fail to disconcert, and which, if disturbed, would be fatal to the means of prosecuting it. Our national government is in its infancy. The habits and dispositions of our people are ill suited to those liberal contributions to the treasury, which a war would necessarily exact. There are causes which render war in this country more expensive, and consequently more difficult to be carried on, than in any other. There is a general disinclination to it in all classes. The theories of the speculative, and the feelings of all, are opposed to it. The support of public opinion (perhaps more essential to our gov-. ernment than to any other) could only be looked for in a war evidently resulting from necessity.

These are general reasons against going into war. There are others, of a more particular kind. To the people at large the quarrel would be apt to have the appearance of having originated in a desire of shielding Spain from the arms of Britain. There are several classes of men to whom this idea would not be agreeable, especially if the Dutch were understood to be in conjunction with the British. All those who were not friendly to our late Revolution would certainly dislike it. Most of the descendants of the Dutch would be unfriendly to it. And let it not be overlooked, that there is still a considerable proportion of those who were firm friends to the Revolution, who retain prepossessions in favor of Englishmen, and prejudices against Spaniards.

7

In a popular government especially, however prejudices like these may be regretted, they are not to be excluded from political calculations.

It ought also to be taken into the account, that by placing ourselves at this time in a situation to go to war against Great Britain, we embark with the weakest party—with a total uncertainty what accession of strength may be gained—and without making any terms with regard either to succor, indemnity, or compensation.

France is the only weight which can be thrown into the scale, capable of producing an equilibrium. But her accession, however probable, ought not to be deemed absolutely certain. The predominant party there may choose to avoid war as dangerous to their own power. And if even obstacles should not arise from that quarter, it cannot be foreseen to what extent France will be in condition to make efforts. The great body of malcontents comprehending a large proportion of the most wealthy and formerly the most influential class—the prodigious innovations which have been made—the general and excessive fermentation which has been excited in the minds of the people— the character of the prince, or the nature of the government likely to be instituted, as far as can be judged prior to an experiment—do not prognosticate much order or vigor in the affairs of that country for a considerable period to come.

It is possible, indeed, that the enthusiasm which the

transition from slavery to liberty may inspire, may be a substitute for the energy of a good administration, and the spring of great exertions. But the ebullitions of enthusiasm must ever be a precarious reliance. And it is quite as possible that the greatness, and perhaps immaturity, of that transition, may prolong licentiousness and disorder. Calculations of what may happen in France must be unusually fallible, not merely from the yet unsettled state of things in that kingdom, but from the extreme violence of the change which has been wrought in the situation of the people.

These considerations are additional admonitions to avoid, as far as possible, any step that may embroil us with Great Britain. It seems evidently our true policy to cultivate neutrality. This, at least, is the ground on which we ought to stand, until we can see more of the scene, and can have secured the means of changing it with advantage.

We have objects which, in such a conjuncture, are not to be neglected. The Western posts, on one side, and the navigation of the Mississippi, on the other, call for a vigilant attention to what is going on. They are both of importance. The securing of the latter may be regarded in its consequence as essential to the unity of the empire.

But it is not impossible, if war takes place, that by a judicious attention to favorable moments, we may accomplish both by negotiation. The moment, however, we became committed on either side, the advantages of our position for negotiation would be gone. They would even be gone in respect to the party with whom we were in co-operation ; for being once in the war, we could not make terms as the condition of entering it.

Though it may be uncertain how long we shall be permitted to preserve our neutrality, that is not a sufficient reason for departing from it voluntarily. It is possible we may be permitted to persist in it throughout. And if we must renounce it, it is better it should be from necessity than choice ; at least till we see a prospect of renouncing with safety and profit. If the government is forced into a war, the cheerful support of the people may be counted upon. If it brings it upon itself, it will have to struggle with their displeasure and reluctance. The difference alone is immense.

The desire of manifesting amity to Spain, from the supposition that our permanent interest is concerned in cementing an intimate connection with France and Spain, ought to have no influence in the case. Admitting the existence of such an interest, it ought not to hurry us into premature hazards. If it should finally induce us to become a party, it will be time enough when France has become such, and after we shall have adjusted the condition upon which we are to engage.

But the reality of such an interest is a thing about which the best and the ablest men of this country are far from being agreed. There are of this number, who, if the United States were at perfect liberty, would prefer an intimate connection between them and Great Britain as most conducive to their security and advantage ; and who are of opinion that it will be well to cultivate friendship between that country and this, to the utmost extent which is reconcilable with the faith of existing engagements : while the most general opinion is, that it is our true policy, to steer as clear as possible of all foreign connection, other than commercial . . . . .* and in this respect to cultivate intercourse with all the world on the broadest basis of reciprocal privilege.

An attentive consideration of the vicissitudes which have attended the friendships of nations, except in a very few instances, from very peculiar circumstances, gives little countenance to systems which proceed on the supposition of a permanent interest to prefer a particular connection. The position of the United States, detached as they are from Europe, admonishes them to unusual circumspection on that point. The same position, as far as it has relation to the possessions of European powers in their vicinity, strengthens the admonition.

Let it be supposed that Spain retains her possessions on our right, and persists in the policy she has hitherto pursued, without the slightest symptom of

---

* In Mr. Lodge's edition there is no mark of omission.

relaxation, of barring the Mississippi against us; where must this end, and at a period not very distant? Infallibly in a war with Spain, or separation of the Western Country. This country must have an outlet for its commodities. This is essential to its prosperity, and if not procured to it by the United States, must be had at the expense of the connection with them. A war with Spain, when our affairs will have acquired greater consistency and order, will certainly be to be preferred to such an alternative. In an event of this sort, we should naturally seek aid from Great Britain. This would probaby involve France on the opposite side, and effect a revolution in the state of our foreign politics.

In regard to the possessions of Great Britain on our left, it is at least problematical, whether the acquisition of them will ever be desirable to the United States. It is certain that they are in no shape essential to our prosperity. Except, therefore, the detention of our Western posts, (an object, too, of far less consequence than the navigation of the Mississippi,) there appears no necessary source of future collision with that power.

This view of the subject manifests that we may have a more urgent interest to differ with Spain, than with Britain. And that conclusion will become the stronger, if it be admitted, that when we are able to make good our pretensions, we ought not to leave in the possession of any foreign power the *territories* at the mouth of the Mississippi, which are to be regarded as the key to it.

While considerations of this nature ought not to weaken the sense which our Government ought to have of any obligations which good faith shall fairly impose, they ought to inspire caution in adopting a system, which may approximate us too nearly to certain powers, and place us at too great a distance from others. Indeed every system of this kind is liable to the objection, that it has a tendency to give a wrong bias to the Counsels of a Nation, and sometimes to make its own interest subservient to that of another.

If the immediate cause of the impending war between Britain and Spain be considered, there cannot be drawn from thence any inducements for our favoring Spain. It is difficult to admit the reasonableness or justice of the pretensions on her part, which occasion the transactions complained of by Great Britain, and certainly the monopoly, at which these pretensions aim, is entitled to no partiality from any maritime or trading people. Hence considerations, neither of justice or policy, as they respect the immediate cause of the quarrel, incline us towards Spain.

Putting, therefore, all considerations of peculiar good will to Spain or of predilection to any particular connection out of the question, the argument respecting refusal or consent, in the case supposed, seems to stand thus:

The acquisition of the Spanish territories bordering upon the United States, by Britain, would be dangerous to us. And if there were a good prospect that our refusal would prevent it, without exposing us to a greater evil, we ought to refuse. But if there be a considerable probability that our refusal would be ineffectual, and if being so, it would involve us in war or disgrace, and if positive disgrace is worse than war, and war, in our present situation, worse than the chances of the evils which may befall us from that acquisition, then the conclusion would be that we ought not to refuse. And this appears to be the true conclusion to be drawn from a comprehensive and accurate view of the subject; though first impressions are on the other side.

These reflections also may be allowed to come in aid of it. Good or evil is seldom as great in the reality as in the prospect. The mischiefs we apprehend may not take place. The enterprise, notwithstanding our consent, may fail. The acquisition, if made, may, in the progress of things, be wrested from its possessors. These, if pressed hereafter, (and we are willing to accept it,) may deem it expedient to purchase our neutrality by a cession to us of that part of the territory in question, which borders on the Mississippi, accompanied with a guarantee of the navigation of that river. If nothing of this sort should happen, still the war will necessarily have added millions to the debt of Britain, while we shall be recruiting and increasing our resources and our strength. In such a situation, she will have motives of no inconsiderable force for not provoking our resentment. And a reasonable confi-

dence ought to be reposed in the fidelity of the inhabitants of the Western country; in their attachment to
the Union; in their real interest to remain a part of it,
and in their sense of danger from the attempt to sepa-
rate, which, *at every hazard*, ought to be resisted by
the United States.

It is also to be kept in view, that the *same* danger,
if not to the *same* extent, will exist, should the territories in question *remain in the hands of Spain*.

Besides all this, if a war should ever be deemed a
less evil than the neighborhood of the British in the
quarter meditated, good policy would still seem to require, as before intimated, that we should avoid putting ourselves in a situation to enter into it, till we
had stipulated adequate indemnities and considerations
for doing so; that we should see a little further into
the unravelment of the plot, and be able to estimate
what prospect there would be by our interference of
obviating the evil. It deserves a reflection, that if those
territories have been once wrested from Spain, she will
be more tractable to our wishes, and more disposed to
make the concessions which our interests require, than
if they never passed into other hands.

A question occurs here, whether there be not a
middle course between refusal and consent; to wit, the
waiving an answer, by referring the matter to further
consideration. But to this there appear to be decisive
objections. An evasive conduct in similar cases is
never dignified—seldom politic. It would be likely to

give satisfaction to neither party—to effect no good—
to prevent no ill. By Great Britain it would probably
be considered as equivalent to a refusal—as amount-
ing to connivance by Spain—as an indication of timidity by all the world.

It happens that we have a post on the Wabash, down
which river the expedition, it is presumable, must go.
If the commannding officer at that post has no orders
to the contrary, it will be his duty to interrupt the
passage of the British troops; if he does, it would seem
necessary for them, in order to the safe passage of their
boats, with their artillery, stores, provisions, and bag-
gage, to take that post. Here then would be a passage
through our territory, not only without our permission,
but with the capture of a post of ours, which would be
in effect making war upon us. And thus silence, with
less dignity, would produce the same ill consequence
as refusal.

If, to avoid this, private orders were to be sent to
the commanding officer of that post, not to interrupt
the passage, his not being punished for his delinquency
would betray the fact and afford proof of connivance.

The true alternative seems to be, to refuse or consent: and if the first be preferred, to accompany it with
an intimation, in terms as free from offence as possible,
that dispositions will be made to oppose the passage,
if attempted to be forced; and accordingly, as far as
practicable, to make and execute such dispositions.

If, on the contrary, consent should be given, it may

deserve consideration whether it would not be expedient to accompany it with a candid intimation that the expedition is not agreeable to us, but that thinking it expedient to avoid an occasion of controversy, it has been concluded not to withhold assent. There are, however, objections to this mode. In case of consent, an early and frank *explanation should be given* to Spain.

QUESTION THE SECOND.—" What notice ought to be taken of the measure, if it should be undertaken without leave, which is the most probable proceeding of the two?"

If *leave* should be *asked* and *refused*, and the enterprise should be prosecuted without it, the manner of treating it has been anticipated; that is, the passage, if practicable, should be opposed; and if not practicable, the outrage should be resented by recourse to arms.

But if the enterprise should be undertaken without *asking* leave, which is presumed to be the import of the question, then the proper conduct to be observed will depend upon the circumstances.

As the passage contemplated would be by water, and almost wholly through an uninhabited part of the country, over which we have no *actual* jurisdiction, if it were unaccompanied by any violence to our citizens or posts, it would seem sufficient to be content with remonstrating against it, but in a tone that would not commit us to the necessity of going to war; the objections to which apply with full force here.

But if, as it is to be feared will necessarily be the case, our post on the Wabash should be *forced*, to make good their passage, there seems to be no alternative but to go to war with them, unwelcome as it may be. It seems to be this, or absolute and unqualified humiliation; which, as has been already noticed, is in almost every situation a greater evil than war.

In every event, it would appear advisable immediately to convene the Legislature; to make the most vigorous measures for war; to make a formal demand of satisfaction; to commence negotiations for alliances; and if satisfaction should be refused, to endeavor to punish the aggressor by the sword.*

ALEXANDER HAMILTON,
Secretary of the Treasury.

---

* The opinion of Hamilton is of special interest, as he had held some informal interviews with Major Beckwith upon the attitude of the United States towards Great Britain in this Spanish affair. The negotiation of Gouverneur Morris at London had reached the ears of Lord Dorchester, presumably in some official manner, and may have suggested to him the expediency of sending a similar agent to New York to sound the American Executive upon certain questions then pending between England and the United States, in which the interests of Canada were involved. Beckwith was the agent selected, and on the 8th of July he held his first communication with Hamilton, and proved that he had a full acquaintance with Morris's mission, and expressed the belief that the British Cabinet was disposed to enter into an alliance, as well as friendly intercourse, with the United States. This led up to a suggestion on Beckwith's part, that, if war should occur between England and Spain, it would be for the interest of the United States to take part with the former power. The points in dispute between the United

States and England were touched upon, and Indian hostilities disavowed by Lord Dorchester. The tenor of Beckwith's communication,
based as it was upon a letter from Lord Dorchester, was such as to
convey the impression that it was not made without some knowledge
and probable suggestion on the part of the English Cabinet.

Hamilton noted down the main points of this conversation, and submitted them to the President and Jefferson. The first views of the
latter have already been given in these pages (p. 65, *ante*), but they
were more distinct and sharply defined in this draft than as afterwards
expressed. In the draft he says the alliance proposed "would involve
us against France and Spain; and, considered even in a moral view, no
price could repay such an abandonment of character." In the completed paper this is toned down to "as to an alliance, we can say nothing till its object be shown, and that it is not to be inconsistent with existing engagements." But all agreed that in the event of war the
United States expected to be strictly neutral.

With this opinion, Hamilton again met Beckwith on the 22d of July.
As the British agent had no particulars of an alliance to offer as the
basis of a negotiation, Hamilton said that "the thing is in too general
a form to admit of a judgment of what may be eventually admissible or
practicable. If the subject shall hereafter present itself to discussion in
an authentic and proper shape, I have no doubt we shall be ready to
converse freely upon it. And you will naturally conclude that we shall
be disposed to pursue whatever shall appear, under all circumstances,
to be our interest, as far as may consist with our honor. At present, I
would not mean either to raise or depress expectation.

"Major Beckwith seemed to admit that, as things were circum-
stanced, nothing explicit could be expected, and went on to make some
observations, which I understood as having for object to sound whether
there existed any connection between Spain and us; and whether the
questions with regard to the Mississippi were settled.

"Perceiving this, I thought it best to avoid an appearance of mystery,
and to declare without hesitation,

"'That there was no particular connection between Spain and the
United States within my knowledge, and that it was matter of public
notoriety, that the questions alluded to were still unadjusted.'"

Mr. Douglas Brymner, the courteous archivist of the Dominion of Canada, informs me that the letters of Major Beckwith to Lord Dorchester on his American mission are still in existence, but not in a condition in which they are available. I am therefore unable to give the Major's versions of these conversations.

When, in October, Hamilton received the decree of the French Assembly addressed to Spain (page 26, *ante*), he thought that " though of a qualified tenor," it looked " pretty directly towards the eventual supporting of Spain."—*Hamilton to Washington*, 17 October, 1790.

WAR OFFICE, 29 August, 1790.

SIR: In answer to your secret communication of the 27th instant, and the questions stated therein, I humbly beg leave to observe,

That the United States, by not being under the obligation of any treaty, either with Spain or England, are in a situation, to grant, or deny, the passage of troops, through their territory, as they shall judge fit.

The granting or refusing therefore the expected demand of a free passage to the troops of England, through the territory of the United States, in order to attack the dominions of Spain upon the Mississippi, will depend upon a due estimation of the consequences arising from either alternative.

The United States are too well aware, of the great and permanent evils, which would result from England's becoming possessed of the Mississippi and West Florida, to concur in any arrangements to facilitate that event.

The law of nations establish the principle, that every neutral nation may, refuse the passage of troops through its territory, when such passage may tend to its injury.

In the present case, the passage of the British troops, would be to effect an object directly contrary to the

(103)

interests and welfare of the United States. If therefore the demand should be made, it may be refused,
consistently with the principles of self preservation,
and the law of nations.

But there are two modes of refusal. A denial unaccompanied by any other act; and a denial accompanied by force to oppose the passage, if it should be
attempted, after having been refused.

The first mode is all that can with propriety be done
in the present state of things. If after the denial, the
british troops should proceed, they become the aggressors, and establish a just cause of war, whenever the
interests of the United States shall dictate the measure.
Although a denial, unaccompanied by any other act,
might be unpleasant to great Britain, yet she would
not probably think it, of itself, a sufficient cause for
waging war against the United States. But if a force
should be actually opposed to the passage of the
troops, a war with great Britain would appear to be
the inevitable and immediate consequence.

The true interests of the United States dictate a
state of neutrality in the affairs between Spain and
England. Should the United States be dragged into
the war in the present moment, the loss of their commerce might justly be expected; the source of their
revenue would be cut off, and the proposed system of
public credit fatally postponed, if not entirely blasted.
These are serious evils and to be avoided if possible.

It is however to be remarked that it is highly improbable that Spain would enter into the war, unless she expected to be supported by France. Nor does there appear any solid objections to the expectation, but the present debilitated and convulsed state of France. The family compact and other treaties between the two kingdoms will continue to exist, notwithstanding the situation of France, until formally renounced. This has not been the case. The probability therefore is, that France will be combined with Spain.

If this should be the case, every effort on the part of France will be employed to associate America in the war. And it is a question of great moment whether the United States could strictly comply with the treaty of friendship and commerce entered into with France on the 6th of February, and observe an exact neutrality.

Although it would seem hardly possible that either England, or France and Spain combined, would make such offers to the United States as to counter-balance the advantages of Neutrality, yet the case may be otherwise, or the United States may be so obliged to enter into the war in order to avert a greater evil.

These considerations with their extensive relations unite in dictating an answer to Lord Dorchester in terms as little exceptionable as possible.

That the United States had recently manifested their sincere desires, not only to continue at peace with Great Britain, but to cement the same by com-

8

mercial arrangements which might be reciprocally beneficial.

But that the real causes of dispute between England and Spain were too little understood at present by the United States for the President to consent to a measure which would seem to be inconsistent with that strict neutrality the United States would desire to observe.

But if notwithstanding this answer, or if no request should be made for the purpose, and the troops march through the territory of the United States, to attack the dominions of Spain, it might be proper for the President of the United States to convene immediately the legislature, if the occasion should be so urgent as to require their meeting at an earlier day than the adjournment, and to lay the whole affair before them, with his opinion of the measures to be pursued. For the Congress are vested with the right of providing for the common defence, and of declaring war, and of consequence they should possess the information of all facts and circumstances thereunto appertaining.

In the mean time the dispositions and designs of the contending parties will unfold themselves. The terms of each side be known and estimated, and the United States better able than at present to judge of the exact line of conduct they ought to pursue.

I have the honor with perfect Respect to be Sir Your humble Servant   H. KNOX.

The President of the United States.

INDEX.

www.ingramcontent.com/pod-product-compliance
Lightning Source LLC
Chambersburg PA
CBHW030547270326
41927CB00008B/1549